Arts as Education

Edited by Merryl Ruth Goldberg and Ann Phillips

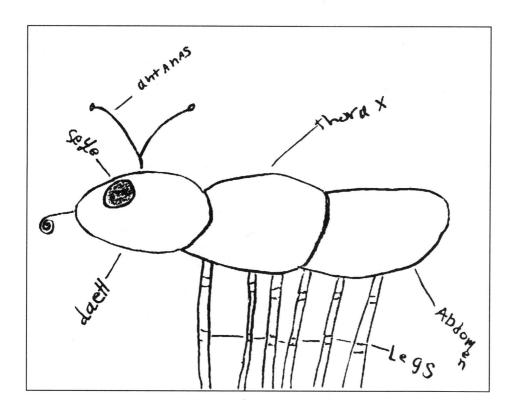

Reprint Series No. 24 / Harvard Educational Review

Library of Congress Catalog Card Number 92-072985

ISBN 0-916690-26-1

Harvard Educational Review
Gutman Library Suite 349
6 Appian Way
Cambridge, MA 02138

Cover Design: David Ford
Photographs: Dody Riggs
Typesetting: Sheila Walsh

Arts as Education

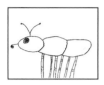

Introduction   *v*
MERRYL RUTH GOLDBERG
ANN PHILLIPS

Texts and Margins   *1*
MAXINE GREENE

Arts as Epistemology:
Enabling Children to Know What They Know   *19*
KAREN GALLAS

To Arrive in Another World:
Poetry, Language Development, and Culture   *33*
JUDITH WOLINSKY STEINBERGH

The Uses of Folk Music
and Songwriting in the Classroom   *55*
VICTOR COCKBURN

Tribal Rhythms: A Thematic Approach
to Integrating the Arts into the Curriculum   *67*
BARBARA BECKWITH
W. THOMPSON GARFIELD
CHARLES M. HOLLEY
J. CURTIS JONES
SUSAN E. PORTER

Working from the Inside Out:
A Practical Approach to Expression   *79*
MARGOT GRALLERT

Computer-Aided Collaborative Music Instruction   *91*
JAMES A. HOFFMANN

And Practice Drives Me Mad;
or, the Drudgery of Drill   *103*
V. A. HOWARD

ESSAY REVIEW
Progressive Journeying   *115*
KATHLEEN MURPHEY
GARY DeCOKER

BOOK REVIEW
Music, Mind, and Education by Keith Swanwick   *125*
MARIE F. McCARTHY

Book Notes   *137*
MERRYL RUTH GOLDBERG

Resource Guide   *153*

About the Editors   *164*

About the Contributors   *165*

Introduction

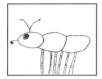

The publication of *Arts as Education* celebrates our belief that the arts are an essential aspect of human development — that is, of knowing and being in the world — and, further, that the arts are fundamental to education. With a reminder to the educational community that it is inclined to sweep aside the arts, we want to begin a new conversation about the importance of the arts in education with the aim of facilitating and changing public discussion about the arts. To achieve that aim, we present the voices of practitioners who view the arts as central to their teaching.

For both teachers and students, the arts can be a form of expression, communication, imagination, observation, perception, and thought. The arts are integral to the development of cognitive skills such as listening, thinking, problem-solving, matching form to function, and decisionmaking. They inspire discipline, dedication, and creativity.

The arts give rise to many voices. They can nurture a sense of belonging, of community; or, they can foster a sense of being apart, of being an individual. The arts also provide a vehicle for individuals, communities, and cultures to explore their own world and journey to new ones, thus enriching their understanding of the varied peoples and cultures that exist on our planet. We believe this is particularly important during this period of global change.

Arts as Education includes the articles from a two-part symposium presented in the February and August 1991 issues of *HER*, along with reviews of books on arts and education and an extensive arts resource guide, which lists books and recordings recommended by the authors and editors, arts journals, and arts organizations. We hope that this collection will bring the arts from the margins to the center of educational discussions and open new conversations about teaching and learning at a time when public policy threatens to limit artistic freedom and the presence of the arts in the schools.

In the first essay, "Texts and Margins," Maxine Greene provides an opening through which the reader is invited to enter a discussion of the role of the arts in life and education. In setting a philosophical stage for such discussion and debate, Greene writes, "*Arts as Education* is intended to open perspectives upon art education and upon the lives we share in this culture.

Hoping to challenge empty formalism, didacticism, and elitism, we believe that shocks of awareness to which encounters with the arts give rise leave persons (*should* leave persons) less immersed in the everyday, more impelled to wonder and to question."

Following Greene's essay, Karen Gallas describes and analyzes the central role of the arts in her first-grade classroom in "Arts as Epistemology: Enabling Children to Know What They Know." "What we understood from our experiences with the arts," writes Gallas, "was that knowing wasn't just telling something back as we had received it. Knowing meant transformation and change, and a gradual awareness of what we had learned."

Poet and teacher Judith W. Steinbergh, in her essay "To Arrive in Another World: Poetry, Language Development, and Culture," offers her perspective as a writer-in-residence and shares with the reader many of her students' poems. Drawing on the diversity of cultures and languages within the schools where she works, Steinbergh and her students explore issues and themes in their lives through writing and reading poetry. "Through the poems read and written in classrooms," Steinbergh writes, "I am allowed entry into children's spiritual lives, their closest relationships, their powerful ambivalences — in other words, into the core that drives their thinking and development." Victor Cockburn, folk-song writer and musician, gives his insights into folk-song writing with children in "The Uses of Folk Music and Songwriting in the Classroom." Cockburn argues that folk songs "have always been an excellent vehicle for storytelling and teaching."

The book continues with four provocative and lively essays. W. Thompson Garfield, Charles M. Holley, J. Curtis Jones, and Susan E. Porter are developers of Tribal Rhythms and senior staff associates of Cooperative Artists Institute, which is based in Jamaica Plain, Massachusetts. Along with coauthor Barbara Beckwith, they describe their work as an interracial company of professional artists in "Tribal Rhythms: A Thematic Approach to Integrating the Arts into the Curriculum." The Tribal Rhythms foursome work within schools as educational strategists "to help schools deal with urgent problems facing today's children, including family fragmentation, loss of community, social and racial isolation, low self-esteem, and deteriorating academic achievement." With the theme of "tribe," the artists attempt to give teachers and students a "framework in which cooperative learning, community spirit, democratic values, self-esteem, and multicultural understanding can thrive."

Next, Margot Grallert, art consultant at an alternative public elementary school in Acton, Massachusetts, describes an art program she defines as "Working from the Inside Out: A Practical Approach to Expression." The philosophy of the school revolves around a belief "that every person has an inner sense of self that can and must provide direction for learning" and that the environment can stimulate the "individual to find his or her own personal direction," and also around a "conviction that there are no final answers." Grallert describes how the arts have been integrated into the everyday curriculum of this alternative school and have become an essential aspect of teaching and learning there.

In "Computer-Aided Collaborative Music Instruction," James A. Hoffmann, a teacher at the New England Conservatory of Music in Boston, Massachusetts, describes a unique harmony class that he has developed. His class format is based on collaborative learning, in which harmony is experienced and learned with the assistance of a computer. Hoffmann argues that the use of the computer has broad implications beyond the learning of harmony, including bringing the roles of composer, performer, and audience closer together. And in "And Practice Drives Me Mad; or, the Drudgery of Drill," philosopher and musician V. A. Howard gives readers a view of the virtues of practice and practising and how important their relationship is to educating the imagination.

Also included in this book is an essay review, "Progressive Journeying" by Kathleen Murphey and Gary DeCoker, which critiques Howard Gardner's *To Open Minds: Chinese Clues to the Dilemma of Contemporary Education*; a related critique by Merryl Goldberg of the book *Artistic Intelligences* (edited by William Moody and based on Gardner's work) appears in the Book Notes section. Marie McCarthy reviews the book *Music, Mind, and Education* by Keith Swanwick, and numerous Book Notes highlight recent books relating to the arts and education.

Finally, we have included an extensive resource guide that provides readings and recordings for readers interested in further exploration of the arts as education. The listings were compiled with the assistance of the book's authors and other contributors too numerous to mention individually, to whom we are deeply grateful. We are especially grateful to Dody Riggs, whose thoughtful editing and devotion to this project have sustained and moved us throughout the entire process.

All the contributors to this book are dedicated to the arts' essential role in teaching and learning. As editors, our hope is that this book will serve to be a resource and inspiration for artists, teachers, learners, policymakers, researchers, philosophers, and theorists, so that the arts will become an integral aspect of ongoing educational practice and debate.

MERRYL RUTH GOLDBERG
Harvard Graduate School of Education and
Wheelock College, Boston, Massachusetts

ANN PHILLIPS
Brookline (Massachusetts) Public Schools

The editors appreciate the contribution of former *HER* Board Members Catherine Lacey, Jayminn Sanford, and Ramón J. Bucheli M. to the early stages of this project.

Texts and Margins

MAXINE GREENE

We are reminded by the critic Denis Donoghue of how many people still consider the arts to be mere entertainments, without practical use. "It is true enough that the arts will not cure a toothache," he says, "nor help very much in surmounting the pressures placed on us by the material world." He goes on:

> But in another way, they are really momentous, because they provide for spaces in which we can live in total freedom. Think of it as a page. The main text is central, it is the text of need, of food and shelter, of daily preoccupations and jobs, keeping things going. This text is negotiated mostly by convention, routine, habit, duty, we have very little choice in it. So long as we are in this text, we merely coincide with our ordinary selves. If the entire page were taken up with the text, we would have to live according to its non-conventional rhythms, even in our leisure hours; because they too are subjected to conventions. (1983, p. 129)

The arts are on the margins, he concludes, and "the margin is the place for those feelings and intuitions which daily life doesn't have a place for and mostly seems to suppress." And finally: "With the arts, people can make a space for themselves and fill it with intimations of freedom and presence" (p. 129). The idea of making spaces for ourselves, experiencing ourselves in our connectedness and taking initiatives to move through those spaces, seems to me to be of the first importance. Some of what this signifies is suggested by Martin Heidegger when he writes about how things happen now and then "beyond what is" when an open place appears: "There is a clearing," he said, "a lighting" reaching beyond what we are sure we know (1971, p. 53).

This book addressing "Arts as Education" is intended to open perspectives upon art education and upon the lives we share in this culture. Hoping to challenge empty formalism, didacticism, and elitism, we believe that shocks of awareness to which encounters with the arts give rise leave persons (*should* leave persons) less immersed in the everyday, more impelled to wonder and to question. It is not uncommon for the arts to leave us somehow ill at ease, nor for them to prod us beyond acquiescence. They may, now and then, move us into spaces where we can create visions of other ways of being and ponder what it might signify to realize them. To say "we" in this fashion is to suggest the existence of a community of educators committed to emancipatory pedagogy, now in the domain of the arts. Such a community would have to include in its dialogue women and men of all classes, backgrounds, colors, and religious faiths, each one free to speak from a distinctive perspective, each one reaching from that distinctive perspective towards the making of some common world. And it would have to be a community *sharing* unabashed love for the arts.

To move into those spaces or clearings requires a willingness to resist the forces that press people into passivity and bland acquiescence. It requires a refusal of what Michel Foucault called "normalization," the power of which imposes homogeneity, allows people "to determine levels, to fix specialties, and to render the differences useful by fitting them one to another" (1984, p. 197). To resist such tendencies is to become aware of the ways in which certain dominant social practices enclose us in molds or frames, define us in accord with extrinsic demands, discourage us from going beyond ourselves, from acting on possibility. In truth, I do not see how we can educate young persons if we do not enable them on some level to open spaces for themselves — spaces for communicating across the boundaries, for choosing, for becoming different in the midst of intersubjective relationships. That is one of the reasons I would argue for aware engagements with the arts for everyone, so that — in this democracy — human beings will be less likely to confine themselves to the main text, to coincide forever with what they are. The "main text" may be conceived as the ordinary, the everyday. It may refer to what Foucault describes as "normalization," or to what is worthy or respectable. Most commonly, what is worthy or respectable is identified with the White, middle-class values so long taken for granted as "American." Because they have been taken for granted, they have seldom been named; therefore they have not been subject to examination or critique. The effect on the minorities, those made to feel like outsiders, is to make them feel "invisible" in the sense that Ralph Ellison uses the term in *Invisible Man*: "That invisibility to which I refer occurs because of a peculiar disposition of the eyes of those with whom I come in contact" (1952, p. 7). When Herbert Marcuse speaks of the qualities of art that allow it to indict established reality and evoke images of liberation, he may be suggesting the relevance of art when it comes to overcoming invisibility.

When I ponder such engagements with works of art, I have in mind those works considered to belong to the "artworld"; it is important to take heed of Arthur Danto's reminder that "there cannot be an artworld without theory, for the artworld is logically dependent upon theory" (1981, p. 135). An art theory can, he says, detach objects from the real world and make them "part of a different world, an *art* world, a world of *interpreted* things." It is a constructed world, therefore, to be viewed as provisional, contingent, and always open to critique. It is also to be regarded as one always open to expansion and revision. The canon, defined by a certain number of men in time past, must always be skeptically conceived and kept open to what has, for generations, been ignored. My concern, however, is not solely with enabling persons to engage authentically and adventurously with a range of work. I also have explorations of media in mind: paint, pastels, clay, engraving stone. I have written and spoken language in mind: the stuff out of which poems are made and stories and riddles, the material through which dreams can be told, fictions invented, novels given form. I think of musical sounds as well: the melody, the dissonance, the pulse of sounds that compose the audible. And I think of dance: of the body in motion with its almost infinite capacity of making shapes, exerting effort, articulating visions, moving in space and time.

Pluralities of persons can be helped to go in search of their own images, their own visions of things through carving, painting, dancing, singing, writing. They can be enabled to realize that one way of finding out what they are seeing, feeling, and imagining is to transmute it into some kind of content and to give that content form. Doing so, they may experience all sorts of sensuous openings. They may unexpectedly perceive patterns and structures they never knew existed in the surrounding world. They may discover all sorts of new perspectives as the curtains of inattentiveness pull apart. They may recognize some of the ways in which consciousnesses touch and refract and engage with one another, the ways in which particular consciousnesses reach out to grasp the appearances of things.

When this happens to people, even very young people, they are clearly more attuned than they would otherwise be to grasping Alvin Ailey's reaching for a celebration at a riverside, Eva Luna's weaving of tales in Isabel Allende's novel *Eva Luna* (1989), Stravinsky's rendering the dash and shimmer of a firebird, Toni Morrison's searing exploration in *Beloved* (1987) of what it might be like to be a mother and to sacrifice and to stand over the abyss, Keith Haring's stark shapes, or the related works of graffiti artists on city doors and walls. Learning the language of Ailey's dance by moving as Ailey dancers move, entering the symbol system of novel writing and story weaving by composing one's own narrative out of words, working with glass sounds or drums to find out what it signifies to shape the medium of sound: all these lead to a participant kind of knowing and a participant sort of engagement with art forms themselves. Aesthetic education includes adventures like these, as it involves intentional efforts to foster increasingly informed and ardent encounters with art works. Not incidentally, it involves the posing of the kinds of questions — aesthetic questions — that arise in the course of art experiences (Why do I feel spoken to by this work, excluded by that? In what sense does this song actually embody Mahler's grief? What is it about the "Ode to Joy" that makes me feel as if I am coming in touch with some transcendent reality? In what way does Marques's novel reflect, refract, explain, interpret Colombian history? In what sense is Jamaica Kincaid's West Indian island "real"?). To pose such questions is to make the experiences themselves more reflective, more critical, more resonant; and if anything, art education as it is usually understood is deepened and expanded by what occurs.

The point of both undertakings is to release persons to be more fully present to an Edward Hopper city painting, a Cézanne landscape, a jazz piece, a Bela Bartók folk song, a Joyce novel. This, in part, is what leads me to propose that art education be infused with efforts to do aesthetic education. By art education I mean, of course, the spectrum that includes dance education, music education, the teaching of painting and the other graphic arts, and (I would hope) the teaching of some kinds of writing. By aesthetic education I mean the deliberate efforts to foster increasingly informed and involved encounters with art works that often free people to be fully present to a Cézanne, an Ailey, a Stravinsky, a Joyce. To be fully present depends on understanding what is there to be noticed in the work at hand, releasing imagination to create orders in the field of what is perceived, allowing feeling to inform and illuminate what is there to be realized, to be achieved. I should like to see one pedagogy feeding into the other: the pedagogy that empowers students to "create," the pedagogy that empowers them to attend and, perhaps, to appreciate. I should like to see both carried on with a sense of both learner and teacher as seeker, questioner, someone "condemned to meaning" (Merleau-Ponty, 1967, p. xix), and reflecting on the choosing process, turning towards the clearing that might (or might not) lie ahead. The ends in view are multiple, but they surely include the stimulation of imagination and perception, a sensitivity to various modes of seeing and sense-making, a grounding in the situations of lived life.

Most agree today that we are unlikely to come upon a fixed definition of "Art" or a theory that accounts for all the art forms that have been and all that have yet to be. Most would support Herbert Marcuse, however, in his claim that art "breaks open a dimension inaccessible to other experience, a dimension in which human beings, nature, and things no longer stand under the law of the established reality principle." The languages and images in works of art, when persons are released to attend and let their energies go out to them, "make perceptible, visible, and audible that which is no longer, or not yet, perceived, said, and heard in everyday life" (1977, p. 72).

We can all recall experiences that validate what Marcuse wrote. I remember, for example, the subversion of traditional orders of reality accomplished by Braque and Picasso when they enabled so many to realize the significance of looking through multiple perspectives at the lived world. I remember the astonishing disclosures offered through the showing of ten or so serial visions of Rouen Cathedral rendered by Monet over three months, now viewed all together. Like the poplar trees or the grain stacks also painted serially by Monet, the cathedral paintings reveal the changing shapes and even the changing meanings of the structure as the times of day change, the play of shadows, the slants of light. In the case of the grain stacks, we may feel a kind of shifting rhythm of relationship, an expressive rhythm, a play between a small and modest grain stack and a looming, protective one, between the shadow cast by the stacks and the glow of the sky beyond. It is not only seeing something in the visible world that we could not have suspected were it not for Monet (and, perhaps, never have tried to render for ourselves); it is also recognizing that the vision — and the meaning and the pulsation — are functions of a certain way of attending on our part. Monet did not, after all, provide for us a window on a series of landscapes that were objectively out there and objectively "impressionist" in appearance. Just as in the case of poetry, meanings are ways of relating to things. The meanings of those Monet landscapes (like Velasquez's *Pope Innocent* or Edward Hopper's lonely city streets or Goya's *Disasters of War*) do not reside in the subject matter, in the canvas on the wall, or in our subjectivities when we come to them. Meaning *happens* in and by means of an encounter with a painting, with a text, with a dance performance. The more informed the encounter — by some acquaintance with the medium at hand, and by some use of critical lenses, some consciousness of an "artworld" (Danto, 1981, p. 5) — the more we are likely to notice, the more the work is likely to mean. If the questions beat inside us, questions about whether or not something is to be called good art or bad art, what context has to do with it, what constitute good reasons, we are likely to wonder and to perceive even more.

None of this could happen, however, without the release of imagination, the capacity to look *through* the windows of the actual, to bring "as/ifs" into being in experience. Imagination creates new orders as it brings, according to Virginia Woolf, "the severed parts together" (1976, p. 72): imagination connects human consciousness and works of visual art, literature, music, dance. Imagination may be the primary means of forming an understanding of what goes on under the heading of "reality"; imagination may be responsible for the very texture of experience. Once we do away with habitual

5

separations of the subjective from the objective, the inside from the outside, appearances from reality, we might be able to give imagination its proper importance and grasp what it means to place imagination at the core of understanding. Hart Crane, the American poet, spoke of imagination as "a reasonable connective agent toward fresh concepts, more inclusive evaluations . . ." (1926, p. 35). In his turn, the poet Wallace Stevens talked about the way imagination enhanced the sense of reality, about it being "the power of the mind over the possibilities of things" (1965, p. 31). Mary Warnock writes of how imagination is connected with feelings or emotions, and how necessary it is "for the application of thoughts or concepts to things" (1978, p. 202). She writes of the need to acknowledge that imagination and the emotions, including taste and sensibility, can be, and ought to be, educated. My argument here is that a powerful way of educating them is through initiation into the artistic-aesthetic domains.

Without imagination, and for all his scientific intentions with respect to the effects of light on appearances, Monet could not conceivably have seen the facade of Rouen Cathedral in so many ways: as a stern embodiment of a dark faith; as a dancing radiant screen of promise; as a delicate lacy veil. Nor could we, without some capacity to transform those strokes of paint, those whites and golds and dark blues into (what?) a rendering of a cathedral, realize that distinctive vision within our consciousness. By doing so, we are very likely to change some dimension of our perceiving, some dimension of our lives.

Wallace Stevens's poetry exemplifies this with peculiar acuity, perhaps especially to those who have themselves tried to write poems. The children Judith Steinbergh writes about, especially Jenny Lusk-Yablick, are discovering dimensions of their own experience even as they are learning to engage with poetry. It is interesting to find this child summoning memories and heirlooms as she (like Stevens) makes a poem of a "lord of sound." Steinbergh stresses "respect for craft," and that summons up V. A. Howard's complex concern for "practising" and "practice." When Stevens compares imagination to a "blue guitar" that (to the despair of certain listeners) does not "play things as they are" (1964, p. 165), he cannot but evoke a resonance in those who know what it is to look at things as if they could be otherwise, and can at once attend to the oddity of a guitar colored blue with strings that can sound an infinity of songs. When Stevens writes of "six significant landscapes" and, letting his imagination play, realizes unexpected possibilities in blue and white larkspur at the edge of a shadow, or in a pool shining "like a bracelet/Shaken in a dance," or in the moon folded in a white gown "Filled with yellow light . . . Its hair filled/with certain blue crystallizations/ From stars/Not far off" (1964, pp. 73–74), he creates new connections between selves and things. He maps even readers' landscapes anew. There follow two even more remarkable verses, reminding readers of shaping, sculpting in a space behind grape leaves, reminding us in climax of what it can signify to look beyond:

> Not all the knives of lamp-posts,
> Nor the chisels of the long streets,
> Nor the mallets of the domes
> And high towers
> Can carve
> What one star can carve
> Shining through grape-leaves.
> (1964, pp. 74–75)

It is not necessary to be a sculptor to share the feeling of discovering by entering a new space — now bringing together knives, chisels, and mallets so that the star itself can become a carver, a sculptor, shining through leaves. It is not only the starlight glimmering and outlining the grape leaves that may be changed through such figurative work. So may the idea or the image of the sculptor, the one who makes unpredictable forms. In the last stanza of the poem, Stevens lets meaning like this culminate somehow and explode:

> Rationalists, wearing square hats,
> Think, in square rooms,
> Looking at the floor,
> Looking at the ceiling.
> They confine themselves
> To right-angled triangles.
> If they tried rhomboids,
> Cones, waving lines, ellipses —
> As, for example, the ellipse of the half-moon —
> Rationalists would wear sombreros.
> (1964, p. 75)

All this, too, is wrought by means of metaphor and through the kind of disclosure of unexpected relationships that brings something new into a reader's world. Experiencing it either from outside or within, the reader cannot but feel released from confinement and from a type of one-dimensionality, both of which depend on the rationalists' gaze. When they are challenged to try rhomboids and cones, they are being lured to allow the lines and squares to move through a spectrum of shapes to the ellipse of the half-moon. They may exchange their mortarboards for sombreros, at least now and then, but they are not being asked to give up thinking or attending to their texts. They are being challenged to do those things with a greater sense of play and of panache, of the dialectic of moon and square room, margin and text.

Explorers of the "Arts as Epistemology," like Karen Gallas and her students, are doing just that. Juan's praying mantis and the children's discovery of the life cycle of the tree are illumined by the imaginative. They are thinking, they are coming to know. And the coming to know is fed by their glimpses of the half-moon.

Most people can summon up kindred examples if we allow ourselves occasional adventures on the margins, if we let ourselves cut free from anchorage through choice and action, through "belonging to the world" (Merleau-Ponty, 1967, p. 456). I am not suggesting that engagements with the arts ought to lead to denials or distractions from the work that has to be done. Nor am I suggesting that the margins are places for giving way to indulgence, to sensuous extremes. As I view them, the arts offer opportunities for perspective, for perceiving alternative ways of transcending and of being in the world, for refusing the automatism that overwhelms choice.

The alternatives may be grim and, at first glimpse, ugly. They may be like the images in Elizabeth Bishop's "Night City":

> No foot could endure it,
> shoes are too thin.
> Broken glass, broken bottles,
> heaps of them burn. . . .
> (1983, p. 167)

And where the tears and guilt are burning, there is a tycoon who "wept by himself" and "a blackened moon." But this is a view from a plane, we are reminded, through a dead sky; and the poem ends hauntingly and with a parenthesis: "(Still, there are creatures,/careful ones, overhead./They set down their feet, they walk/green, red; green, red.)" (p. 168).

Like the violated children in Charles Dickens's novels, the battered women in Charlotte Perkins Gilman's works, the little ones tormented in Dostoyevsky's world (where, as Ivan Karamasov tells his brother, "It is a peculiar characteristic of many people, this love of torturing children and children only" [1945, p. 286]), like the guerrilla fighters being executed in *Disasters of War*, like the photographs of scenes from the Holocaust, there are images and figures that speak directly to our indignation, to some dimension of ourselves where we connect with others. They open our eyes, they stir our flesh, they may even move us to try to repair.

I recently saw a painting of the German terrorist, Ulrike Meinhof, fallen on her back after what seems to have been her hanging. Her dim pallid profile and her wounded neck appear in an airless setting where there is neither clarity nor breathing space. The painter is Gerhard Richter, who worked from photographs in his rendering of the *Red Battalion* — all of whom are now dead. "Art," he wrote, "is always to a large extent about need, despair, and hopelessness . . . and we often neglect this content by placing too much importance on the formal, aesthetic side alone" (quoted in Kuspit, 1990, p. 129). Donald Kuspit comments that the "dialectic of concreteness and hazy suggestiveness" in this dim depiction of photographed reality

> emphatically articulates the major fact about the deaths: their incomprehensibility, the suspicion that surrounds them. . . . This is what makes them catalytic of "infinite," morbid speculation, including pessimistic observation of how seemingly "open" images of events can in effect be used to rewrite history by closing it down. This incomprehensibility issues in the slippery, hidden mood of the paintings. (pp. 131–132)

Richter himself apparently sees all ideologies and many beliefs as life-threatening, and he regarded the Baader-Meinhof gang as victimized by ideological behavior per se. We look, we wonder, and the questions come and batter us. We might think of Walter Benjamin writing of the mangled body as object, of the age of "mechanical reproduction" and the self-alienation to which it leads (1978, pp. 217–251). He spoke of our inability to incorporate technology, of war being a rebellion of technology collecting "in the form of 'human material,' the claims to which society has denied its natural material. Instead of draining rivers, society turns a human stream into a bed of trenches; instead of dropping seeds from airplanes, it drops incendiary bombs . . ." (p. 242). Images like Richter's may perhaps evoke that kind of outrage; that may be what ideology and terror finally ask of us — along with a fundamental doubt, a responsiveness to pallid pointless death.

I am trying to say that one of the functions of the arts is not only to make us see (as Joseph Conrad wrote) "according to our deserts" (1897/1960, p. 30), not only to change our everyday lives in some fashion, but to subvert our thoughtlessness and complacencies, our certainties even about art itself. Prone as we are to oppose aesthetic experience to the controls and limitations imposed by technicism, we may be too likely to find occasions for shelter in the arts, mere fulfillment of unmediated desire. Because so many of our faces are turned towards children whose spontaneity we want so badly to preserve, we choose too frequently to find purity and radiance in domains that touch the depths as well as the heights of being human in the world.

It is because I believe it is so important for those of us who teach to be reminded of this that I value encounters with artists like Joseph Beuys so much, and with Robert Wilson, and Philip Glass, and William Balcon, and Toni Morrison, and Martha Clarke, and John Quare. Their association with the avant-garde or the postmodern is not the important thing. Apart from the complex quality and, often, the eerie beauty of their works, there is the problematic each embodies, the restiveness with limits, the peculiar sense of some approximation of "the ellipse of the half-moon." I think, for example, of Jenny Holzer and her mobile neon messages sculpting the spirals of the Guggenheim Museum not long ago — red, white, like electric signs, with the phrases and the words colliding, overlapping, the meanings rising and fall-ing. There are truisms spelled out by the electric bulbs and inscribed on marble stools, truisms sometimes as vague as Richter's images, sometimes startlingly and embarrassingly clear. There are one-liners: "The Family is Living on Borrowed Time," "Abuse of Power Comes as No Surprise," paro-dies and simplifications, once on the walls of buildings and bus stops, now in distinguished museums (Waldman, 1989). Most recently, her work has been at the Venice Biennale, where it won a first prize. There are what she calls "Laments," introspective in the first person: "With only my mind to protect me I go into Days"; "What I fear is in a box with fur to muffle it. Every day I do nothing important because I am scared blank and lazy" (p. 18).

I watch them move by, become cliché, become collage, become concep-tual art, minimal art. I watch a language of signs rendering the visible world invisible at a moment when I am celebrating the slow emergence of my world into visibility. "I try not," Holzer says, "to make it completely random or sloppy, but there still has to be a wild part in it. In the writing you have to go off into the stratosphere and then come back down. That's what I like, when things spin out of control but then are pulled back so that they're available to you. I want them to be accessible, but not so easy that you throw them away after a second or two" (Waldman, 1989, p. 15). Appreciative as I am of her moving between randomness and control, of her using language to move beyond the tangible, I am caught in questions again about meaning and reference, and I find the questions almost as important as the moments of disclosure. Some of the same questions arise, I realize, when I try to penetrate the mythic, the secret parts of Toni Morrison's *Beloved* or go back to William Faulkner's "The Bear," or try to discover (at this late date) what Herman Melville really intended by "the whiteness of the whale," or what "confidence" and "trust" actually signified in his strange story called "The Confidence Man."

Of course we need to use criticism, if only to help us elucidate, to help us notice what is there to be noticed, but we also have to find out what the critics individually assume, as we have to look from various critical vantage points at works we are trying to make clear. We have at once to resist the pull of expertise, and to be conscious of "hype" and fetishization and the ways in which the market determines value and choice. Today we who are teachers have an obligation to be aware of and wary of efforts to determine from above (or from some apocryphal center) what is acceptable in the world of art and what has to be branded unacceptable because it is charged with being pornographic, impious, homosexual, unpatriotic, or obscene. To issue edicts like the ones we have recently read, to utter proscriptions and prescriptions may be within the law. If, however, we stand by the view that experience always holds more than can be predicted, and that imagination creates openings to the unpredictable, we cannot but be chilled by what the recent prohibitions imply. Realizing, too, that creative and appreciative encounters in the domains of the arts depend upon imaginative energies, we can only anticipate a lulling and a limiting consequence — miseducative in the deepest sense. We are bound to ponder as authentically and critically as we can what a Robert Mapplethorpe exhibition means to us as persons and what its banning means. The same is true with regard to Andres Serrano and Karen Finley and those who burn the flag. And it might well have been true when *Marat/Sade* and the musical *Hair* presented frontal nudity upon the stage. We do not necessarily want to expose children to Mapplethorpe or Finley, although there may well be ways of doing so. We do, however, want to learn ourselves — and enable them to learn — what it is to make judgments on the grounds of lived experience and, at once, in relation to community norms. Trying to open persons to the new and the multiple, we want ourselves to break through some of the crusts of convention, the distortions of fetishism, the sour tastes of narrow faiths.

This requires us to be in continuing quest of ourselves, even as it requires that we do what we can to enable as many of the young as possible to crack the codes that prevent so many of them from engaging with works of art. Paintings, novels, works of music are not likely to be realized by untutored consciousnesses if they are made to appear in enclaves, out of reach, in an esoteric or somehow timeless realm. John Dewey said that works of art are too frequently presented as if they have no roots in cultural life, as if they are specimens of fine art and nothing else. Art objects are made to seem remote to ordinary people, as are many fine fictions and music that reaches beyond the accustomed horizons of sound. Set on pedestals, actual or figurative, art forms are removed "from the scope of common or community life" (Dewey, 1934, p. 6). Because they are deliberately set apart from ordinary experience, they serve largely as "insignia of taste and certitude" (p. 9). They confirm people in their elitism; they serve the interests of social power. Walter Benjamin, with somewhat the same idea in mind, wrote of concepts like eternal value and mystery, and used the word "aura" to signify a distance, a uniqueness, as well as an embeddedness in tradition (1978, pp. 222–223) that made art works inaccessible to the mass of people. John Berger writes about the ways in which works of art are "enveloped in an atmosphere of entirely bogus religiosity. Works of art are discussed and presented as though they were holy relics: relics which are first and foremost evidence of their own survival" (1984, p. 21). Later, he makes the point that the visual arts have always existed in a preserve, magical or sacred or physical, and that later "the preserve of art became a social one. It entered the culture of the ruling class, while physically it was set apart and isolated in their palaces and houses.

During all this history, the authority of art was inseparable from the particular authority of the preserve" (p. 33).

There is not only the distance established by those locating art forms in a "preserve" of some kind; there is the distance created by commodification, by esotericism, by false claims of "realism," by mystifications having to do with women, people of color, the poor, and the excluded. There is also the separation caused by innocence, by lack of knowing, by a reliance upon the uninformed, the innocent, or those conditioned by the media. Nor are the arts likely to open themselves naturally to young people who have been systematically demeaned, excluded from what others think to be the "goods" of their own world. John Berger argues strongly against the view that the arts can be understood spontaneously. He writes:

> The idea of innocence faces two ways. By refusing to enter a conspiracy, one remains innocent of that conspiracy. But to remain innocent may also be to remain ignorant. The issue is not between innocence and knowledge (or between the natural and the cultural) but between a total approach to art which attempts to relate it to every aspect of experience and the esoteric approach of a few specialized experts who are the clerks of the nostalgia of a ruling class in decline. (In decline not before the proletariat, but before the new power of the corporation and the state.) The real question is: to whom does the meaning of the art of the past properly belong? To those who can apply it to their own lives, or to a cultural hierarchy of relic specialists? (1984, p. 32)

This leads back to my argument for a pedagogy that integrates art education and aesthetic education. Yes, it should be education for more informed and imaginative awareness, but it should also be education in the kinds of critical transactions that empower persons to resist both elitism and objectivism, that allow them to read and to name, to write and to rewrite their own lived worlds.

It is clear enough, of course, that there can be great enjoyment of pieces of music, paintings, film, dance performances, and (to a lesser extent) literary works grasped in moments of immediacy, without the interaction of outer and inner visions so essential if works of art are to be brought fully alive. It is clear enough, as well, that there is always a danger of imposing alienating standards, of suggesting a single "right" way of looking at a Monet poplar painting, of discerning the mirrored king and queen behind the artist in Velasquez's always problematic *Las Meninas,* of making sense of the "madwoman" in *Jane Eyre,* of interpreting the film called *The Third Man* in one particular way. To take an opposing view and teach with the suggestion that it is all, in any case, subjective, "a matter of taste," would be equivalent to the kind of permissivism that leads to a mindless relativism. To assume, for instance, that nothing is missed if we attend the ballet *Giselle* and wait simply for the "story" to unfold, for Giselle to go mad and be abandoned, is to lose the possibility of an aesthetic experience with the dance called "Giselle." To judge the worth of *War and Peace* by its fidelity to the Napoleonic Wars, or of *A Streetcar Named Desire* by its fidelity to New Orleans or the "truth" it tells about some kinds of pathology, is again to avoid the aesthetic potentialities in each work, to refuse the illusion, to treat it as just another window on the world.

Dewey used to remind his readers of how necessary it was for their imaginative and perceptual energies to reach towards a painting or a poem if it were to be transmuted into an aesthetic object *for* the one perceiving it. He continued to insist that the aesthetic is not an intruder from without, not an affair "for odd moments" (1934, p. 54). Like many others, he used the example of a crowd being conducted rapidly through a gallery by a guide. Donoghue has similar images in mind when he speaks of the "cherishing bureaucracy" and the temptation to assimilate, manage, or domesticate the arts (1983, p. 71). As he sees it, the "State" or those in control seem to be saying that artists can do what they like, because nothing they do makes any difference to anyone (p. 74). And, indeed, they will not make any real difference if people rush by paintings, go into reveries in concert halls, skim through works of fiction, come in contact with art forms only from the outside, as if the works in the various domains were indeed commodities. Dewey wrote about how important it always is to *attend* actively, to pay heed, to order the details and particulars that gradually become visible the more we look into integral patterns — what Dewey called "experienced wholes." He said:

> There is work done on the part of the percipient as there is on the part of the artist. The one who is too lazy, idle, or indurated in convention to perform this work will not see or hear. His "appreciation" will be a mixture of scraps of learning with conformity to norms of conventional admiration and with a confused, even if genuine, emotional excitation. (1934, p. 54)

There might be recognition, he said, an attaching of correct labels, but there would not be the energizing encounter that counteracts passivity. There would not be the launching of persons into the making of meanings, the grounded interpretations or "readings" that make for wide-awakeness. Most of us recognize the delicate balance that must be achieved between the spontaneity of the initial response (perhaps the "careless rapture" of that response) and the "work" that is so necessary if the painting, dance, or fiction is to be realized. What we as teachers can communicate about that work and the energies to be released are the crucial issues, not necessarily the importance of cultural literacy or an adeptness at identifying great artists and works of art. Learning to overcome passivity and induration, learning to notice what is to be noticed may lead on and on to new disclosures. I think of Jean-Paul Sartre saying this so clearly with regard to literature: If the reader, he wrote, "is inattentive, tired, stupid, or thoughtless, most of the relations will escape him. He will never manage to 'catch on' to the object. . . . He will draw some phrases out of the shadow but they will seem to appear as random strokes" (1963, p. 43). When we read at our best, he suggested, we project beyond the words a theme, a subject, or a meaning. We realize through the language something that is never given *in* the language, whether it is an Emily Dickinson poem or a Sartre play. And, later, we are helped to see that the artist tries to oblige the reader or the percipient to create what he/she (the artist) discloses, to become an accomplice in freedom with that artist, an accomplice in releasing possibilities. It is this sort of action that is at the core of aesthetic education, this sort of action that may (it seems to me) save our human lives.

V. A. Howard's cautionary voice and reminders of the importance of "initiating into a trading by aspiration, demonstration, and precept" may be another way of saying this. He is talking about the discipline of growing *into* our traditions and the freedom of moving beyond them. In his essay, too, there is a sense of predicament, of a dialectic, and — through hard work — a possibility of breaking free.

If we can enable more young persons to arouse themselves in this way, to notice, to make sense of what they see and hear, to attend to works in their particularity, they may begin to experience art as a way of understanding. If we distinguish between the analytic, abstract rationality we often associate with knowing and the peculiar relational activity that brings us personally in touch with works of art, we might even call art — as Karen Gallas does, though from a different vantage point (that of the maker or creator) — a way of knowing. The experience-knowledge gained by this way of knowing means opening new modalities for us in the lived world; it brings us in touch with what Merleau-Ponty called our "primordial landscapes," where we were present at the moment "when things, truths, values" came into being for us, when we were present at the "birth of knowledge" and recovered the "consciousness of rationality" (1964, p. 25).

Since encounters with the arts can never be end-points, they may challenge us to new encounters in experience. We may have the experience Merleau-Ponty described when he talked about "a route" being given to us, "an experience which gradually clarifies itself, which gradually rectifies itself and proceeds by dialogue with itself and with others" (1964, p. 21). It is hard for me to conceive of a better argument for the relevance of the arts in schools — if it is indeed the case, as so many people believe, that boredom and a sense of futility are among the worst obstacles to learning. To feel oneself en route, to feel oneself in a place where there are always the possibilities of clearings, of new openings: this is what we hope to communicate to the young, if we want to awaken them to their lived situations, enable them to make sense, to name their worlds.

The philosopher Charles Taylor finds a way of saying this with regard to realist painting in his book, *Sources of the Self* (1989). Such painting, he writes, brings to the fore

> patterns, lines of force, whole aspects of things, which are certainly there in our visual field, but overshadowed, made recessive, by our normal ways of attending to and apprehending things. There is a vast latent content to our awareness of things and indefinite multiplicity of patterns only tacitly there, unthematized relations in what is called our pre-objective world. (p. 468)

He is talking about a retrieval, a recovery of lived experience and the meaningful forms and relationships that undergird our ordinary perception and are so often simply ignored. Painters like Cézanne and Frida Kahlo were able to convert into visible objects that which would have, without them, remained walled up in the separate life of each consciousness. Writers like Virginia Woolf can make us "see" in such a fashion that — as she herself put it — we are no longer "embedded in a kind of nondescript cotton wool" (1976, p. 70), but are enabled to experience "moments of being" that might have been impossible were it not for the arts. Toni Morrison, at a different moment and in another space, enables us to achieve as meaningful, against our own lived experience, the tragedy of Pecola Breedlove in *The Bluest Eye* (1972) when she writes: "A little black girl yearns for the blue eyes of a little white girl, and the horror at the heart of her yearning is exceeded only by the evil of fulfillment" (p. 158). Once again, things hidden are revealed, at least to those willing to break with "induration" and try to "catch on." Again, that is one of the concerns of aesthetic education: to enable people to uncover for the sake of an intensified life and cognition. It also becomes an argument for opening the self to other ways of seeing, other ways of speaking — to the art forms of other cultures, and the stories, and the sounds. Victor Cockburn's use of folk music and songwriting suggests openings for understanding diverse and distinctive ways of being in the world.

At the heart of what I am asking for in the domains of art teaching and aesthetic education is a sense of agency, even of power. Cockburn's notion of the power of folk music "as a means of individual expression and a tool for social change" suggests possibilities in the many domains of the arts. Painting, literature, theatre, film; all can open doors and move persons to transform. We want to enable all sorts of young people to realize that they have the right to achieve works of art as meaningful against their own lived lives. Because the world that the arts illumine is a shared world, finally, because the realities to which they give rise emerge through acts of communication, the encounters being sought are never wholly autonomous or private. Moving from our own explorations of pictorial space to a conscious encounter with a Braque painting, looking up from our own effort to make a poem to a Robert Frost or a Muriel Rukeyser poem — we can always enter into dialogue with those around. The languages can be explored; the reasons given; the moments of epiphany celebrated; the differing vantage points articulated. Communities of the wide-awake may take shape, even in the corridors of schools.

If we are indeed to make the margins visible and accessible, if we are to encourage dialectic movements from margin to text and back, we ought to open larger and larger meeting places in schools. We ought to reach out to establish ateliers, studios, places where music can be composed and rehearsed, where poems and stories can be read. There might be new collaborations among questioners, as teachers and students both engage in perceptual journeys, grasp works and words as events in contexts of meaning, undertake common searches for their place and significance in a history to which they too belong and which they invent and interpret as they live.

What we are about must be, can be life-enhancing, as more and more living beings discover what it is to make a shape, an image, to devise a metaphor, to tell a tale — for the sake of finding their own openings into the realms of the arts. No matter how alienating, how shocking some of the images and affirmations they confront (and are urged to confront), they must learn that they can never be equated with actualities like war-wounded children, young men left broken on the side of the road, bodies scarred by torturers, the eyes of people behind bars. These are horrors too often evaded, denied, or taken for granted by those willing to remain passive, to coincide forever with themselves. So I end with a heralding of more shocks of awareness as the time goes on, more explorations, more adventures into meaning, more active and uneasy participation in the human community's unending quest.

References

Allende, I. (1989). *Eva Luna*. New York: Bantam Books.

Benjamin, W. (1978). *Illuminations*. New York: Schocken Books.

Berger, J. (1984). *Ways of seeing*. London: Penguin Books.

Bishop, E. (1983). *Collected poems*. New York: Farrar, Straus & Giroux.

Conrad, J. (1960). Preface to "The nigger of Narcissus." In J. E. Miller, Jr., *Myth and method*. Omaha: University of Nebraska Press. (Original work published 1897)

Crane, H. (1926, October). *Poetry*, p. xxix.

Danto, A. (1981). *The transfiguration of the commonplace*. Cambridge, MA: Harvard University Press.

Dewey, J. (1934). *Art as experience*. New York: Minton, Balch.

Donoghue, D. (1983). *The arts without mystery*. Boston: Little, Brown.

Dostoyevsky, F. (1945). *The brothers Karamasov*. New York: Modern Library.

Ellison, R. (1952). *Invisible man*. New York: Signet Books.

Foucault, M. (1984). The means of correct training. In P. Rabinow (Ed.), *The Foucault reader*. New York: Pantheon Press.

Heidegger, M. (1971). *Poetry, language, and thought*. New York: Harper & Row.

Kuspit, D. (1990, April). All our yesterdays. *Artforum*, pp. 129–132.

Marcuse, H. (1977). *The aesthetic dimension*. Boston: Beacon Press.

Merleau-Ponty, M. (1964). *The primacy of perception*. Evanston, IL: Northwestern University Press.

Merleau-Ponty, M. (1967). *Phenomenology of perception*. New York: Humanities Press.

Morrison, T. (1972). *The bluest eye*. New York: Pocket Books.

Morrison, T. (1987). *Beloved*. New York: Alfred A. Knopf.

Sartre, J-P. (1963). *Literature and existentialism*. New York: Citadel Press.

Stevens, W. (1964). *Collected poems*. New York: Alfred A. Knopf.

Stevens, W. (1965). *The necessary angel*. New York: Vintage Books.

Taylor, C. (1989). *Sources of the self*. Cambridge, MA: Harvard University Press.

Waldman, D. (1989). *Jenny Holzer*. New York: Harry N. Abrams.

Warnock, M. (1978). *Imagination*. Berkeley: University of California Press.

Woolf, V. (1976). *Moments of being*. New York: Harcourt, Brace, Jovanovich.

Arts as Epistemology: Enabling Children to Know What They Know

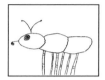

KAREN GALLAS

One afternoon in early June, six children and I crowd around a butterfly box watching a painted lady chrysalis twitch and turn as the butterfly inside struggles to break free. Juan, who is seated on a chair next to the box, holds a clipboard on his lap and is carefully sketching the scene. This is his third sketch of the day chronicling the final stage in the life cycle of the butterfly. It will complete a collection he began in early May, when mealworms arrived in our first-grade classroom. As he draws, the children agonize over the butterfly's plight. They have been watching since early that morning, and they all wonder if the butterfly will ever get out. Sophia smiles to herself and then begins to hum a tune.

"I'll sing it out," she says.

"Yeah, let's sing it out!" agrees Matthew, and all of the children begin to improvise a song. Juan looks up, smiles, and continues to sketch.

Events such as these have become almost commonplace in my classroom. Over the course of the school year, this class of children questioned, researched, wondered, and discussed their way through a wide variety of subject matter and concepts. What distinguished their learning process from that of many other children, however, was the presence of the arts as an integral part of their curriculum: as a methodology for acquiring knowledge, as subject matter, and as an array of expressive opportunities. Drawing and painting, music, movement, dramatic enactment, poetry, and storytelling: each domain, separately and together, became part of their total repertoire as learners.

By describing the development of a unit on insects, this article will show how the arts can play an essential role in forming and extending all aspects

Harvard Educational Review Vol. 61 No. 1 February 1991

of a curriculum. The concept of life cycles, which informed our study throughout, was the focus of several months of work for my first-grade class. Eighteen children, from a range of socioeconomic, racial, and cultural backgrounds, and including four different language groups, participated in this study from late winter through the month of June. What happened in this class could happen in any class of children. Each group brings a wide range of life experience to school, and, though we are often initially separated by language, culture, and racial barriers, I have learned that the creative arts, rather than labeling our differences, enable us to celebrate them.

Juan arrived in September from Venezuela, speaking no English but filled with joy at being in school. As I struggled during our first few weeks together to find out what he could and could not do (and found out that, according to my teacher's agenda, he could not do many things), Juan very graciously attempted to help me understand what he could do. He would tolerate a few minutes of my informal assessment activities and then use his one word of English: "Paint?" he would suggest cheerfully, and by that time I would agree. "Paint," for Juan, meant drawing, painting, modeling, or constructing, and it was his passion. As the weeks passed, I continued to be amazed by his talent and frustrated by his inability to learn the alphabet and basic readiness skills. However, Juan's own nonchalance about the process of learning to read and write was somewhat contagious, and I began to see that his art was presenting both what he had already learned at home and in school, and what he desired to learn. It soon became clear that our forays into the world of number and letter recognition would be fruitless without Juan's skill as an artist. His visual representations became a catalogue of science information and science questions, and that information began to provide material for his involvement in reading and writing — and learning a new language. As Juan drew, we built a reading and speaking vocabulary from his pictures, and that vocabulary, together with his interest in representing science, also became the subject matter of his writing.

Juan was teaching me once again a lesson that I seem to have to relearn each year: when given the opportunity, listen to the children. They will show you what they know and how they learn best, and often that way is not the teacher's way. Because I am a teacher, my unspoken agenda is shaped by academic expectations: I am supposed to present concepts and skills, and the children are supposed to "master" those skills and concepts. Unfortunately, the journey towards mastery of a subject is often inextricably tied to instruments of assessment, presentation, and communication that are designed by and for teachers. Tests, workbook pages, teacher-led discussions, textbooks, charts — each of these assumes a commonality of experience that the children in a classroom may not share. Each artificially separates the

Illustration by Juan

process of mastery from that of individual expression. Each of these excludes the full participation of some portion of the population I teach.

How do young children convey their understanding of the world around them? Before they begin school, and even in the primary grades, most children depend on play, movement, song, dramatic play, and artistic activity as their means of making sense of the world. That these pastimes gradually give way to predominantly "adult" styles of communication is more a tribute to the power of traditional schooling and parental pressure than a statement of the natural process of expressive maturation. What unfolds each year in a classroom that places the arts as a centerpiece of the curriculum is simply a continuation of the early preoccupations of childhood. Children, unlike most of their teachers and parents, are comfortable using virtually all of the expressive modalities. Because one does not need to teach the "how" of the artistic process to them, their ability to use the arts for their own educational process is expansive.

Developing a multi-arts curriculum allows me to follow the children's own expressive interests while also using the artistic process as an integral part of the identification and expansion of their knowledge in different areas. This method goes beyond the use of art as an enhancement or enrichment of an already established curriculum and places the arts as central to the completion of the curricular process. For both teacher and child, the arts offer an expanded notion of classroom discourse that is not solely grounded in linear, objective language and thinking, but rather recognizes the full range of human potential for expression and understanding.

From the first days of our study of the life cycle of insects, we used basic creative and critical thinking skills to identify our existing knowledge base. What did these children know about insects, and what did they want to know? As a group, we brainstormed, sharing our common knowledge, and in the process generated questions we wanted to answer. Later we drew a semantic map to extend and relate our ideas.

What We Know About Insects	*Questions About Insects*
Birds eat them.	Are caterpillars insects?
They have six legs.	How many legs do beetles have?
Some are furry or slimy.	Do all insects have legs?
Some help trees.	Do all insects fly?
Some fly.	How do fireflies light up?
Some eat fruit.	Why do fireflies light up?
Some people eat them.	How do insects grow?
They could destroy the earth.	How do insects swallow?
Some eat wood.	Do they have teeth?
Some live underground.	How old can an insect get?
Some are dangerous.	How do they smell?
Some insects eat other insects.	How many kinds are there?
Most have antennae.	Do insects have lips?
Some have wings and don't fly.	Do they all hop?
Some insects are poisonous.	Do they smell with antennae?
Some help plants.	
Some insects eat plants.	
Some insects have stingers.	

Our study then began in earnest with observations of mealworms. We observed, sketched, and took notes on their behavior. Juan discovered in our second day of sketching that one of his mealworms was in the process of shedding its skin. Thus began the first in his series of meticulous sketches, both from live animals and from nonfiction books about insects. As a class, we spent the afternoons in the first week sketching, studying books and photographs, discussing entomological drawings by different artists, and observing the mealworms and caterpillars. On Friday we showed some of the sketches, and talked about what we were learning. The children were very

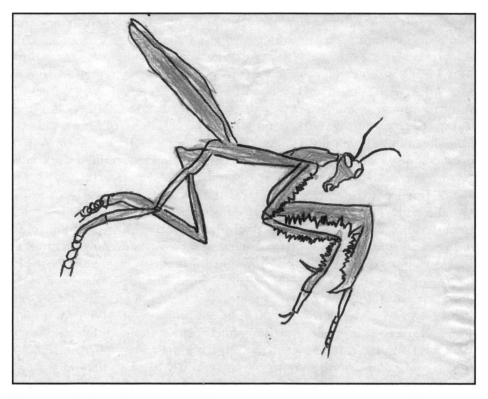

Illustration by David

impressed by the work, and those who hadn't been sketching asked Juan how he got so good.

"I practice a lot," he said, and our discussion continued about why we were sketching.

> *David:* I'd heard people talk about this thing. I think it was a praying mantis, but I didn't know what it was. So I looked at a book, and then I drew it, and then I knew what it was.
>
> *Juan:* Or if you don't know what a wing is and how it's made you can draw it and then you know.

A few days later, Adam was seated by himself, trying to sketch a picture of a monarch butterfly from a book. Since September Adam had struggled with fine motor tasks, such as drawing, cutting, or construction, but he was so impressed with the work of other children that he had decided to try to do a sketch. As I watched, he was quite absorbed and had finished one wing, but the second wing was more difficult. He threw down his pencil, and I could see he was going to cry. "Don't stop, Adam," I said, and he nodded, wiped his eyes, and picked up the pencil.

Juan walked over to see what was wrong and offered a few suggestions. "You don't have to make it perfect today. Just draw it, then do more tomorrow." Adam went back to work. A few minutes later I saw him using the length of his forefinger to gauge how big the wingspread in the picture was. Juan came over to check, but said nothing. Adam continued until it was time to go home, and worked on the picture for another week until it was finished. He had done a beautiful, meticulous job, and he asked if I could make copies for the class to share.

It is intense artistic activity like this that begins in the early stages of learning and continues throughout a study that enables children to become immersed in a subject. The deep involvement in representing the form of an insect, whether it is one that has been observed or one only pictured in books, expands the child's basic knowledge of that organism and his or her ability to represent it both in thought and form. For Juan, visual representation is a natural process. It is his method for examining his world, as well as his means of externalizing what he is learning for others to share. For Adam, who excels in reading, writing, and abstract thought, but who often has a difficult time communicating and interacting with other children, the artistic process of drawing the monarch butterfly expands his own boundaries of symbolic representation and gives him a new way to reach out to other children. Adam often approached the learning process in a highly verbal and discursive manner, delighting in puns and playing on words or ideas in his speech and writing. These abstractions sometimes eluded his classmates, and thus the act of presenting himself in a visually compelling form became a new challenge for him as a learner.

One day early in our study, Carolyn made a special request. She had finished reading most of our nonfiction resource books, but she wanted to know if I had any poems about insects. I was sure I did, but I wondered why. She explained:

> A poem is a little short, and it tells you some things in a funny way. But a science book, it tells you things like on the news. . . . But in a poem, it's more . . . the poem teaches you, but not just with words.

Carolyn, whom I would often find throughout the year alone in the coat-cubbies writing poetry on scraps of paper, had reminded me that I had constructed my plans and gathered my resources too narrowly. Throughout the year as a class, we had used poetry as a way to gain more insight into whatever subject we were studying. Carolyn began to collect poems to read to the class about insects, and I reconsidered the place of poetry in this study. Her interest in metaphoric ways of knowing is not an isolated one. Poetry sometimes provides children with a window of insight that is broader than that offered in even the best nonfiction resources. Poetic form is often more suited to the thinking and writing of children than prose; it is spare, yet rich with sense impressions. It is a medium in which the images of wonder, curiosity, and analogic thinking, which so often characterize children's language, can flourish.

In the next week, our observations of insects continued outside, where each child found an insect habitat, observed the insect, sketched the habitat, and wrote field notes. Upon returning one afternoon, we shared our findings and began to discuss the relationships between our classroom study and our outdoor explorations. Soon after, we read *The Inch Boy* (Morimoto, 1986), a Japanese folk tale that describes the experiences of a character who never grows larger than an inch tall. The children were fascinated by the notion of living in the world as a tiny being. Adam wondered out loud what the world might be like for a tiny velvet spider mite: he had made the connection that I hoped would occur.

Jeffrey offered, "Well, what you might think is a hill would probably only be a pebble or a big piece of dirt."

"And," added Carolyn, "you might never see the blue sky, only just green and green and you'd think the top of the world was green." These ideas produced a lot of commotion, and before we left the meeting I asked the children to write a poem in the persona of an insect that they had observed. Sean chose the ant:

ANT
by Sean

I pretend I'm a ant
running and dodging birds.
Grass feels tickly under my feet.
Big trees shade me.
I climb a bush and I see buildings
houses and even other bugs too.
And then I see a watermelon seed
and I go off to carry it away with my friends.

After two weeks, the mealworms and caterpillars were pupating, and these observations, together with our classroom research and outdoor experiences, offered an opportunity for us to compare the life cycles of several insects. Many children had gained a great deal of new knowledge about different insects and their habits, and their understanding had been shared in a variety of ways. I encouraged the children to relate and expand their knowledge through movement and dramatization. In small groups, they presented either the life cycle of an animal they had observed or one they had researched. Each group conferred, agreeing on an insect to present, and then after some rehearsal mimed the stages of that insect's life cycle. Sometimes each member of a small group enacted a different stage in that cycle, while in other groups the members played out the transformation in unison. Brian and Roberto lay on the floor, legs tucked against their sides, mirroring the slightly visible legs on the mealworm pupa. I was surprised when they portrayed the transition from mealworm to pupa with such accuracy that even the timing of the twitching of the pupa was realistic.

For Brian, who might easily be labeled "attention deficit" because of his constant motion and distractibility, the action and focus of the movement experience demonstrated how carefully he had observed and examined the mealworms, and it also showed that Brian has the ability to translate his ideas into a kinetic modality with great clarity. By offering him access to the arts of movement and enactment, I have been able to see Brian's strengths: how carefully he observes and analyzes every detail of the world around him, and how creatively he solves challenging problems. Those strengths are often obscured by his behavioral problems, but when Brian works through movement and drama, the behaviors that handicap him in one situation become his gifts.

One of the more difficult tasks that I face as a teacher is moving children like Brian beyond the level of acquiring new knowledge and ideas and asking them to synthesize and apply their ideas to new and different contexts. It would be easy for me to take a very basic approach to assessment and simply ask children to regurgitate what they have learned, and we would have reached our goals: "Tell me the facts of the life cycle of insects and label the stages on this diagram." Yet the act of moving beyond simple knowledge acquisition towards true assimilation of learning is the challenge for most children, and the process of assessing their learning in a way that stimulates that growth is my challenge. True knowing means transformation and change, and it is that level of learning that I hope for but often find difficult to offer as a possibility to the children.

Fortunately, however, when given the opportunity, the children will provide me with ideas to accomplish this goal. Sean, who is a talented artist, had become fascinated by the notion of relative size. He asked if he and Jeffrey could do a picture to go with his poem. They spent a week working on a huge mural, drawing towering blades of grass, large rocks, and giant sunflowers, then adding tiny insects trudging up the huge plants. Sean's fascination, like Carolyn's, expanded my ideas of what was possible both for these children to grasp conceptually and for all of us to achieve aesthetically. The union of critical and creative thinking that I had repeatedly observed taking place in the production of the mural, in Sophia's song about the struggle to complete a cycle, in Brian's translation of biological change into movement

Detail of illustration by Sean and Jeffrey

— this interaction that constantly occurs in the process of artistic activity is the key to an expansive curriculum.

Like the children, I must remain open to the potential of the arts to expand both my knowledge of the children I teach and my creative insight into the ongoing development of a curriculum. Many times I seem to miss opportunities to expand the children's experience because I am unable to see beyond the boundaries of my own goals for their learning. For example, Juan, our keen observer, in his careful scrutiny of all the pictures in our resource books, discovered a picture of a cocoon we had had in our room for several months but were unable to identify. The description in the book

confirmed what we had observed in early May, when hundreds of tiny caterpillars came streaming out of the cocoon and then promptly took up resi-
dence in our garbage garden. There they crawled through the planters and
wrapped themselves in pieces of leaves and potato skins. We were astonished
and puzzled. The little caterpillars were, we read, called bagworms. Alison,
who had brought us the cocoon in late winter, was terribly excited about the
discovery. For several weeks we watched the survivors grow amidst the potato
plants, which they preferred. They continued to cover themselves in leaves
and debris.

At the same time, eight children, including Alison, had become involved
in reading and sharing different "why" and "how" stories, such as *Why Mosquitoes Buzz in People's Ears* (Aardema, 1975) and selections from the *Just So
Stories* (Kipling, 1902/1978), which explained occurrences in the natural
world. For me, Juan's discovery of the bagworm and its habits, which struck
us all as ludicrous but wonderful, and the children's interest in stories that
offered humorous explanations of animal adaptation seemed to mesh with
our class discussions of how animals and humans adapt to survive in their
environments.

My realization that these events coalesced also addressed the challenge of
developing an integrated arts curriculum that provides a range of arts experiences that will offer opportunities for *all* children to communicate their
new knowledge and expanded understanding of the world. Every child is not
a visual artist, like Juan or Sean, though some are; every child does not find
expanded meaning through the poetic voice like Carolyn, though many do;
and every child cannot represent an idea in movement or sound, like Brian
and Roberto. The challenge, then, is to ensure that the range of experiences
is broad enough to reveal each child's voice, and that those experiences
spring from events that all of the children have shared in common.

Alison, whose shy demeanor and sparse language gives an impression of
austere silence, is, in fact, a storyteller. Storytellers are often unknowingly
discovered (and then eschewed by teachers) in the daily classroom event of
sharing time. Their talents are rarely recognized in a classroom, because talk
and telling is generally dominated by the teacher. Yet storytelling, as we know
from studies of culture and folklore, is a way to pass on knowledge and
information, and is a dramatic event. Like drawing, music, and movement,
it is also a preferred medium through which some children more adeptly
clarify their relationship to the world and to their companions.

When I placed the challenge before the children of taking their new knowledge about insect life cycles and applying it to a different problem, Alison
decided, with a few other children, that she wanted to make up a story to
tell the class. Her story would explain how the bagworm came to carry the
bag. At the same time, several other children decided to invent completely

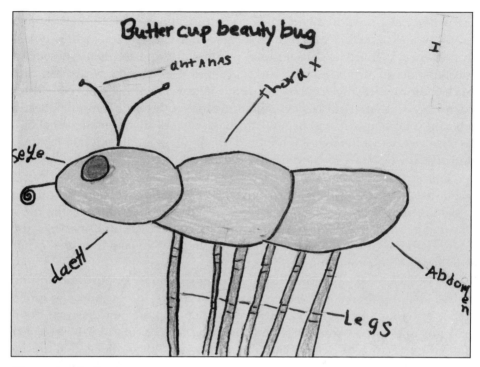

Illustration by Ronit

new insects based on their generalized knowledge of insects and draw or construct their imaginary habitat and life cycle. Alison proceeded to write a twelve-page story about the bagworm, which she edited and revised, realizing at one point that she had forgotten to explain allegorically that the female bagworm never comes out of the bag. When she finished, she told us a story in which the bagworm went from a tiny, unnoticed nuisance to a huge creature that ate everything in sight. In order to save themselves from the wrath of humans, the female worms decided to construct a bag to hide in, and they invited the males to join them. "But," said Alison in conclusion, "the males only stayed in the bags until they turned into moths, but the females were too scared to ever come all the way out, so they even laid their eggs inside of the bag, and then they died there." What Alison had described was the correct life cycle of those strange animals, but her vehicle for presenting it was entirely of her own invention. The story enabled her to transform her observations and study of insects, and her involvement with a new literary genre, into a unique language event. In effect, Alison was creating her own folklore about a phenomenon she had observed in the world.

As Alison finished her project, other children created insects that were adapted to completely unique circumstances. I observed Ronit drawing a

picture of her insect. She had labeled it with two parts: "head" and "body."
I saw this and asked her to rethink what body parts an insect had. She looked
at her drawing and back at me, then got up and went to fetch her science
journal, opening it up to refer to a diagram we had used a few weeks earlier
when we observed the mealworm beetles. On a new piece of paper, Ronit
correctly redesigned her insect to include three body parts, colored it in with
a bright yellow crayon, and began a third drawing of the insect in its habitat.
As she drew, she told me it was going to live in the grass when it was an adult,
and that it would get its food from buttercups.

"This is the actual size of my insect," she said as she drew a line which was
about two inches long. Then she stopped, her eyes widened, and she gulped.

"Oops, that's way too big," and she grabbed the eraser once again. After
drawing a line that was much smaller, she continued, "Aren't I smart? 'Cause
I was thinking of him in the buttercups, so I had to make him smaller, or
someone would come along and be terrified."

For Ronit, the art experience at this time became an opportunity to find
out what she did or did not understand and to rethink her ideas in a new
form. Watching her work on an artistic problem, I was able to see that Ronit
had not understood some basic information, but I could also observe her
quickly correcting herself and thinking through the problems that are inherent in this type of activity. An extremely creative child, Ronit's love of
drawing, writing, and language shows great flexibility of thinking and sensitivity to imagery. The art experience in this instance stimulated her to clarify
her basic information while also engaging her aesthetic viewpoint.

Late in June, as we approached the end of school, we talked about our
studies of life cycles. I asked the children to brainstorm with me about what
they thought of when they heard the word "metamorphosis." Here is what
they said:

> *Metamorphosis*
> egg — mealworm — pupa — beetle
> egg — tadpole — frog
> egg — caterpillar — chrysalis — butterfly
> egg — caterpillar — cocoon — moth
> egg — larvae — mosquito
> seed — plant — flower — fruit
> water — rain — snow — ice
> wind — tornado — cyclone — waterspout
> egg — dinosaur — reptile — bird
> egg — baby — grownup — death — dirt

We gathered for a movement and drama session after this, and I asked
the children to describe, through movement, a metamorphosis that they had
thought about or seen. Most of the children presented impressions of one
of the ideas listed above. Finally, Brian, Jeffrey, and Lea, who had asked to

go last, took their turn. They began with Brian enclosed between Lea's and Jeffrey's arms, as if in an embrace. Slowly, Lea and Jeffrey opened their arms and lifted Brian above them with his arms outstretched. He stood there as long as they could hold him and then the three toppled over together, flattened against the ground. Brian leapt up, took out an imaginary pencil, and began to write on Jeffrey's stomach. The other children who had been mystified, jumped to their feet and shouted, "Tree! It's the life cycle of a tree!"

What we all understood by the end of this study was more than a collection of ideas about life cycles. What we understood from our experiences with the arts as subject matter and as inspiration was that knowing wasn't just telling something back as we had received it. Knowing meant transformation and change, and a gradual awareness of what we had learned. For both children and teacher, the arts offer opportunities for reflection upon the content and the process of learning, and they foster a deeper level of communication about what knowledge is and who is truly in control of the learning process. As a pedagogical standard, the integration of the arts offers a rich resource for educators to infuse the learning experience at all levels with expansive and challenging perspectives.

The arts make it possible for all children, regardless of their differences, to participate fully in the process of education. They transcend the limitations placed on those children, like Juan and Brian, whose language, culture, or life experience is outside of the mainstream of American schooling. They challenge children like Adam to expand their boundaries of personal expression and communication. They confirm the perspectives of children like Alison, Sean, and Carolyn, whose modes of communication and expression do not fit the predominant classroom discourse. They enable all children to recognize the breadth and depth of their learning.

References

Aardema, V. (1975). *Why mosquitoes buzz in people's ears.* New York: Dial Press.
Kipling, R. (1978). *Just so stories.* New York: Weathervane Books. (Original work published 1902)
Morimoto, J. (1986). *The inch boy.* New York: Puffin.

To Arrive in Another World: Poetry, Language Development, and Culture

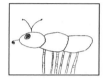

JUDITH WOLINSKY STEINBERGH

Once, before giving a poetry reading, I mentioned that perhaps by age forty we would have enough life experience to qualify to write a poem. "Make that seventy," suggested an older woman in the audience. However, reading and writing poems with children in grades K–12 every day of the school year, I see another side to the matter. While it is true that age and compassion deepen our insights into the poems we read and write, even after nineteen years of teaching I can still be surprised by one child's interpretations of a line of poetry or another's unique view of the world as expressed in an original poem.

As a child, I learned to write verse from my Aunt Fay and my father. By the third grade, I had become a specialist in occasional verse. In adolescence, I delved into "serious poetry" after an encounter with a fourteen-year-old boy who "wrote seriously." A class with Helen Moore at the Ellis School in Pittsburgh introduced me to the poetry of Amy Lowell and led to a love of language that has shaped my adult life.

In 1979, I gradually gave up my position as research economist with a management consultant firm to volunteer in the Cleveland Public Schools. There I developed a program to teach poetry and poetry writing to students in grades K–12. After moving to Boston in 1981, I joined Poets in the Schools, which was directed by poet Ruth Whitman. The group was part of the growing Massachusetts program, Artists in the Schools. Though never trained as a teacher, I found I loved to teach, especially a subject about which I was so passionate. Eventually I acquired teaching certification, and in 1986 I was hired as Staff Writer-in-Residence in the Brookline Public Schools in Massachusetts.

Harvard Educational Review   Vol. 61   No. 1   February 1991

I taught in Brookline three days a week, rotating through the eight elementary schools, and visited the high school briefly each year. I continue to work freelance in other Massachusetts schools through a variety of Arts Council and local grants. This has brought me into urban, suburban, and rural settings, where I have discovered what kinds of poetry and writing exercises succeed in diverse environments.

In a typical week of visiting classrooms, I engage in a range of activities that might include: making up a dance to a rhythmic poem in a kindergarten, acting out short poems in grade one, observing and writing about tadpoles in grade three, discussing and writing poems about families in grade five, writing poems for two voices in grade six, discussing the use of physical objects as symbols for abstract ideas in grade seven, and learning to recognize and write a sonnet in grade eight. I might ask students in English as a Second Language or bilingual classes to write about a place they remember well from their native country, using both their first language and English. In a high school classroom I might discuss poems related to a specific book or a major theme in a literature course the students are taking, or discuss broad themes and styles in poetry from various cultures.

I use a partnership model to work in classrooms. By planning, teaching, and responding to students with the classroom teachers, I have learned what to expect from children at progressive stages of development, and also how poetry ties in with their units in science and social studies, literature and language arts, classroom and global issues. My coteachers have learned how to structure poetry lessons and writing assignments, how to help children transform their vision through art, how to encourage children to take risks in content and in style, and how to guide children to revise their work in a way that integrates craft with the energy of raw expression. The classroom teacher and I, together with the class, offer feedback on students' poems, commending their strengths and urging them to push further with an element of language or content. Since poetry writers often make themselves vulnerable through their personal revelation or individual voice, positive criticism is essential for their continued growth.

An Approach to Writing and Teaching Poetry

My own approach to teaching the reading, discussion, and writing of poetry in grades K–12 has two major components. One is the exploration of source material — the themes and subjects that are sources of inspiration. The second is the communication of poetic writing techniques: the use of sense image, simile, metaphor, persona, parallel structure, poems of address, instruction, rhyme, meter, and syllabics. This approach has evolved from my own process as a writer. I often discuss with students the problems of choos-

Judith Steinbergh reads poetry with members of Ms. Merriman's first-grade class at the Mattahunt School in Mattapan, Massachusetts.

ing topics, focusing on an aspect or moment of the idea, and finding a context for the subject that will give it universal appeal. We also discuss technical issues such as what kind of imagery, diction, rhythm, and form will make the poem successful. The following is an example of how a poem might originate and develop.

When my children were young, I carefully planned their summers to include experiences of ferry rides to Nantucket, blueberry picking in the moors, or rock climbing along the Maine shoreline; I felt I could influence their adult memories. As they moved toward adolescence, however, I could see that their memories from childhood were of the unpredictable, the painful, the bizarre.

When I was ready to write a poem on this subject, and had a stretch of quiet time (maybe a year after I first thought about it), I sat down at the typewriter to begin. But with what? With a blank piece of paper and a phrase, "What memories will rise?", I began to tell the story. I hoped that the techniques I had gathered all my life — the use of image, simile, metaphor, compression of language, an ear for phrasing, knowledge of form — would hover about my head and guide me. Whose voice would I speak in? Whom would I address? What tone would I take? Should I choose a traditional form such as a sonnet, write in free verse, or make up a new form? The form that emerged — rhymed quatrains — seemed to reflect best the subject matter: the plans and hopes that parents impose on their children's lives. The constraints of the form helped to distance me from the intensity of emotions often associated with family issues.

WHAT MEMORIES WILL RISE?

Parents are a strange lot, we make
our children's memories like a quilt,
choosing the fabric and the color. We shape
the pattern. As they grow into adults

we hope they'll wear around them as a charm
the heat of ledgy rocks along the coast,
acres of sharp raspberries at the farm,
the bang of a screen door in the summer dusk.

Will they tell their sons and daughters of the taste
of wild blueberries in a pie,
of the night I woke them and we raced
to see Perseid showers in the sky?

Will the scent of lilac bring them back
to their cluttered dressers full of blooms,
Will they hear their skis in frozen tracks
or see the froth of beach plum over dunes?

What memories will rise like slow whales
breaking the opaque surface of their age,
some boy, we never knew of, who once smiled,
the heartbreak of an empty cage,

the way a face swelled from a sting,
a vision of a car just overturned,
kites lost in trees, birds with broken wings,
how maple leaves shrivel before they burn.

Nightmares, pleasure, passion, they'll forget
the way the ocean ferry soothed their hearts.
What they do remember will be hot,
sweet, bitter, sharp, brilliant as fire sparks.

Judith Wolinsky Steinbergh

The point of all this is that poetry does not just come to you — but neither does a Bach 'cello suite when you first pick up the 'cello. Poetry evolves into a medium of artistic expression as you learn and grow.

What I do with students is first to open up and affirm their vast store of inspiration, and then to help them acquire enough craft to transform their raw material into an art form that others will want to share. This is both challenging and risky. It is *challenging* because our students come from such diverse backgrounds, cultures, economic conditions, abilities, and family values. When they speak of their own lives it informs our learning with new insight and emotion. Through their poetry, I am able to learn what the major themes and issues are for each child, and how these subjects work on the young writers' minds. In this way, I am able to honor the ideas, values, and voice of each child in the classroom.

Yuki is a fourth grader who arrived from Japan in the fall. Her quiet demeanor in class belied her true personality, expressed in this poem, which she wrote in English in April of the same year.

I LIKE TO SPEAK

I like to speak very loud
I like to scream very loud
In Japanese.

I like to laugh very loud.
I like to laugh very loud
In Japan.

I like to sing a song very loud
In anywhere.

Yuki Mori, 4th grade

My work is *risky* because in poetry the creators feel more vulnerable than in any other expressive form — perhaps because they can't hide behind made-up characters or a plot as they can in fiction. I often let students know that I feel very exposed and defensive when I read aloud one of my poems for the first time. I empathize with the risks students are taking and suggest ways in which I might support them. I try to encourage, to teach through positive feedback, to establish an atmosphere of trust and safety. Until students have developed their own confidence to assimilate criticism and rejection, I try to protect them and their developing efforts from ridicule, competition, outside judgment, and censorship.

This poem by seventh-grader Mona Fergus was written with poet Ted Thomas. Mona articulates the dilemma of the adolescent who must present one appearance to her peers while hiding a multitude of feelings and complexities inside:

When I look deep inside,
I see an inner world,

Not expressed to the outer world,
A person that is opposite
of the one I express.
If you were to look deep into me,
You would see the feelings,
the hope,
the sadness,
something hidden by material things,
gold silver,
A heart of love.

Mona Fergus, 7th grade

Poetry and the Developing Child

With poetry, children have a chance to pay attention to their language development, play with words, invent words, make music from phrases, and recognize when they have used figurative language. When a child of three or four says that the moon looks like a fingernail, we say, "Yes, that's terrific!" and think to ourselves, "Wow, this child is already using similes." When the child is five or six, we explain that making these connections or comparisons helps the reader see more clearly what the writer is experiencing. When they are eight or nine, they can grasp that a "comparison" is a "simile," and when they are ten, they learn how to turn it into a metaphor. When they are eleven or twelve, they are able to use the moon as a symbol for stages of the human life cycle or human emotions that wax and wane. By age thirteen or fourteen, they can transform their moon poem into a sonnet or into forms from current culture, such as rap or blues.

The sources and techniques that become evident to students who read and discuss poems can become useful tools when students transfer them to their own writing attempts. Some transfer of skills and subject matter can be made at each grade level. What children are ready to read, to recognize in published poetry, and to transfer to their own poetry writing roughly follows developmental theory. Variations depend on each child's pace of development, teachers, family situation, unique gifts, and engagement in the process of writing.

The following two examples, by a second and a fourth grader, employ a number of techniques not normally expected from children of their age. This level of writing provides evidence that some children speak the language of poetry effortlessly, and can employ sophisticated poetic devices quite early. While I do not wish to push children into forms of expression for which they are not ready, I often introduce poetic techniques a year or two before most of the students in a class are expected to understand them. This challenges the children who are advanced in their expressive language

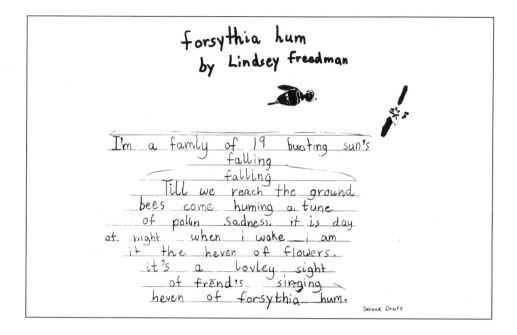

and affirms the gifts of those who think metaphorically or hear their own phrasing and rhythms as they would a song.

This poem by Lindsey, a second grader, was written as she looked carefully at a sprig of newly opened forsythia during a primary science unit:

FORSYTHIA HUM

I'm a family of 19 bursting suns
falling
falling
till we reach the ground,
bees come humming a tune
of pollen sadness. It is day
of night when I wake,
I am in the heaven of flowers,
it's a lovely sight
of friends singing,
heaven of forsythia hum.

Lindsey Freedman, 2nd grade

Lindsey observes that the nineteen individual blossoms on a forsythia branch look like suns bursting. She speaks in the voice of the blossoms (in a persona), which conveys a deeply personal connection to the subject matter. The line "bees come humming" is onomatopoeic. The poem is filled with metaphor: "a tune of pollen sadness," "a heaven of flowers," and the incredible final one, "heaven of forsythia hum." Lindsey has a gift for observation, a feel for cadence, and is willing to take language risks.

Comparing her earlier draft with the final version, we see how close it is in both diction and form. (The line breaks may have been altered slightly and punctuation added during a conference with her teacher or me.) While students can be encouraged to consider suggestions from their peers or teachers, they often have a strong desire to hold on to their original language. Therefore, first drafts are often close to final drafts, especially in content, imagery, and diction. As one sixth grader said, "You write it the way you want it to sound . . . with sound and silence." Another explained, "Even if you change it, you still remember the words that you had before. . . . Sometimes a poem is kind of personal and certain words or certain ways of describing things are part of the poem, not just meanings." In other words, if students change the language too much based on outside suggestions, they lose what they originally heard in their heads — that which is organic to the meaning of their poems.

The following poem, by fourth-grader Jenny Lusk-Yablick, was written about her family's antique trumpet after we had studied some sections of Wallace Stevens's "Thirteen Ways of Looking at a Blackbird." The Stevens poem is difficult and ambiguous, but each section adds another layer to his vision of the blackbird as image and symbol. Here Jenny builds — image by image — a feeling for the antique trumpet which, even as it evolves into a clear object, begins to represent more than the instrument itself: a memory, a family heirloom, a love for music, a respect for craft, and the joy and peace that accompanies the trumpet's long-awaited song:

MY TRUMPET, THE LORD OF SOUND

Two parts big and little.
Two parts silver and gold.
   When placed together
   will make a memory.

The ancient book aside,
The circles and lines spread the page,
   Put these three parts together,
   and a sound you will hear so
   beautiful it could make a vulture sing.

It was an instrument in its time,
but a lord in ours; we long to hear
its royal echoing sound,
   it is a dove flying high,
   a symbol of peace.

Its coffin has two sides,
One of velvet, the other shiny black armor,
Within this shell of night
    our golden dove sleeps, awaits
    its song.

When these four parts are put together,
it awakens.
    Our song has come
    to the trumpet.

Jenny Lusk-Yablick, 4th grade

In the first stanza, the two pieces of the trumpet are able to evoke both a past era and a valued family memory, perhaps of the former owner of the trumpet. The second stanza refers to the antique music book filled with staff and notes. The fourth stanza describes the old case for the trumpet — its outside of shiny armor, the inside of velvet — for which Jenny uses the metaphor "shell of night." In it the trumpet becomes "a golden dove," an extension of the previous stanza's "dove of peace." It is precocious for a fourth grader to be able to understand and transfer some of Stevens's form and technique to her own writing, and this level of accomplishment leads me to believe that poetry reading and writing can push children ahead in language development and abstract thinking.

Poetry and Diversity

Students often study one or more cultures in depth during a school year. The themes and styles of poetry derived from such diverse cultures as Inuit, Native American, African, Japanese, Chinese, Latin American, Middle Eastern, Russian, and Celtic can help students perceive how heritage and language influence thought and expression, while common themes such as family, environment, memories, and dreams connect cultures and the experiences of our students. Growing numbers of our students come from backgrounds where poetry is an integral part of the culture. Hispanic, Russian, and Asian students often feel very comfortable with the expressive mode of poetry, even before they have a facility with English. When children come from a culture where poetry is held in esteem and poetic thinking is as valued as logical thinking, then we must be sure to respect and build on these values.

The following two poems were written by seventh- and eighth-grade Spanish-speaking male students with their bilingual teacher, Maria Marrero. The poems, which are moving and passionate, reflect the poets' Hispanic roots, especially since the writers are at an age when students born in this country value a cool exterior and reserve of feeling. Marrero feels that poetry is the most powerful vehicle for expressing attachments to one's native land and the awe and hardships of finding acceptance in a new country.

EL MUNDO

Al llegar a otro mundo,
es como caer en un
hoyo negro todo sin
color y sin risas.

Es como buscar,
algo que no se
te ha perdido y que
nunca podrás
encontrarlo.

Cada día se va
y ni me doy cuenta,
como se va. Tal vez
se lo lleva el viento,
tal vez no.

Piero Mercanti, 7th grade

THE WORLD

To arrive in another world
is like falling into a
black hole all without
color and without laughter.

It's like looking
for something you
have not lost and
you will never find.

Every day passes
and I can hardly account
for it. Perhaps
the wind takes it,
perhaps not.

translated by Maria Marrero

MI PATRIA

Mi patria, patria de
mi corazón. Recuerdo aquella
vez cuando me fuí sin tu
amor.

Siempre te recuerdo cuando
ando caminando. Recuerdo
cuando caminaba con desencanto.

Oh, patria mi patria
de mi amor yo siempre te he
querido con todo mi corazón.

Ando por la calle pensando
ir para allá. Pero a veces pienso
que alla no encontraré ná

Mi Patria, Patria de mi corazón.

Felix Alonzo, 8th grade

MY HOMELAND

My homeland, homeland of
my heart. I remember that
time when I left without your
love.

Always I remember you when
I go walking. I remember
when I walked with disenchantment.

Oh, my homeland
of my love I have always
loved you with all my heart.

I walk through the street thinking
of going there. But sometimes I think
that there I will find nothing.

My homeland, homeland of my heart.

translated by Maria Marrero

Writing about Family

While language and custom influence literature and thought, broad themes recur in every culture. These themes include: family, memories, dreams, the spiritual life, and the familiar environment. If we look at a selection of poems on the theme of "family," we can see how the concept of "family" is viewed differently in various cultures, but also what common experiences and emotions students have across cultures. Writing about family allows students to examine their relationship to parents, to extended family, and to siblings, to think about what is valued enough to pass along within a family, and to accept the powerful bonds and the ambivalence inherent in family life. In these poems, we see the intensity of feeling expressed by students in grades K–8 from African-American, Hispanic, and other cultural backgrounds about their family lives. In these poems, we see how poetry truly is "the language of the heart."

This poem by a first grader was written using invented spelling just as she began her writing life. She obviously had not been influenced yet by society's stereotypes of grandmothers:

> My grandma is a classy lady,
> She can be mushy sometimes.
> She wears a V-cut sweater
> with bells on it.
> She wears a short, black skirt
> and red high heels.
> All the time she is here
> she is very funny.
>
> *Anonymous, 1st grade*

The poem below was written collaboratively by Ms. Martinez's bilingual first grade. Students listened to a poem, "Abuelita," by Tomas Allende Iragorri, and used his idea of giving imaginary and bountiful gifts to a relative to express the extent of their affection. I asked the children to think about their mothers or someone very close to them, about what they might give to that person to show how deeply they felt. Ms. Martinez translated these questions into Spanish, and the children answered with several ideas. As she wrote these on the board, other children suggested embellishments, such as "con brillo azul y una perla" (with blue shine and a pearl). The poem was completed when Ms. Martinez asked the children, "and what are these gifts for?" "Para hacer feliz a mi mama" (to make my mama happy). "Poetry," Maria Marrero tells her students, "should be in the mother tongue, where we hear the music of the language we are born into."

LE DARÉ MI CORAZÓN

Le daré mi corazón
a mi mamá
Un traje rojo con brillo
azul y una perla
Pondré una estrella que
brille en una caja,
como un arete
Zapatos con hebillas y lazos
para hacer feliz a mi mamá.

The poem was then translated by Ms. Martinez with the students, a lovely and instructive way for students to acquire vocabulary in both languages.

I WOULD GIVE MY HEART

I would give my heart to my mama,
a red dress with blue shine and a pearl.
Put a star that shines in a box for an earring
Shoes with buckles and bows
to make my mama happy.

This next poem by third-grader Chrystal, who is deeply connected to the music of her own voice, was written quickly in class during an exercise to create a family portrait in words. Many students write their first drafts in the form of a paragraph; the final versions differ mainly in line breaks. Chrystal's inner language is so lyrical, the reader can easily hear the music of the poem with its richness of internal rhyme and slant rhyme. The line breaks were suggested to offer the reader clues about where to pause and breathe:

POCKETS FULL OF CANDY

My grandma's a saint with rosy cheeks,
and pockets full of candy
for my brother, my cousins and me.
If you look at her face, you'll see a twinkle of her eye
as she looks back at you
like she's going to cry.
Hands in her pocket,
one comes out with a candy,
then she whispers never shouts,
"this is for you, put it in your mouth"
and then I can't wait . . .
mmmmm that candy's so dandy
my grandma's a saint.

Chrystal Donegan, 3rd grade

> Pockets full of candy.   by Chrystal. D.   Lincoln 3-Reilly
> My grandma's a saint with rosey check's
> and pockets full of candy for my
> brother my cousins and me. If you
> look at her face you'll see
> a twinkle of her eye as looks back
> at you like she's going to cry.
> hands in her Pocket one comes out with
> a candy then she wispers never
> shouts "this is for you put it in
> your mouth" and then I can't
> wait mmm that candy's so dandy
> my grandma's a saint.

Janee, a fourth grader, conveys the intensity of a relationship with her grandmother that is based on family and spiritual connections that are clearly of great value in her culture. Her affection for her grandmother is so great that she can't express it adequately, and so "the privacy of the poem remains" a mysterious yet delicate line that respects family ties:

MY GRANDMOTHER

My grandmother tells lovely stories
and when she sings it fills the hearts
of my cousins and me.
She is the only person who understands
the inside of me. She can easily
stop the tears that sometimes
cover my cheeks. I am glad
she is my grandmother and I love her.
I love her so much
that the privacy of this poem remains.
She has helped me with the word of the Lord
to understand and know.

Janee, 4th grade

Nina Lanza, a fifth grader, chose sewing as the focus for creating a portrait of her mother and exploring her relationship to her mother. The act of learning to sew and even the thread itself become metaphors for the bond between mother and daughter:

MOM

She is at her sewing machine,
The needle goes up and down,
Up and down,
Up and down,
The needle's foot goes up
And she turns the material,
Her brownish-silver hair
  falling forward.
I remember someone saying to her,
  "Where's the wrinkles?"
Her favorite blue sweater looks
  warm and comfortable,
Covered with lint.
"Dinner," I say.
She looks up,
The sewing machine stops,
She takes her glasses off,
Showing her blue-green eyes.
  "Let me finish this."
The threads of the dress seem
  to hold her there.
Sometimes we fight,
And sometimes we're kind.
She teaches me to sew,
So that some day I might be sitting
  there,
Sewing,
Sewing,
As if the threads hold me there.

Nina Lanza, 5th grade

My experience with boys from Spanish-speaking culture, like fifth-grader Edgar Vargas, reveals that they will often write about their mothers without restraint or embarrassment, unlike boys of this age from the United States:

MY MOM

My mom is sweet like sugar to me.
I love her so much like a bear and his honey,
She calls me sweetie,
I call her pretty.
When I come, I kiss her there,

and when I go, I miss her everywhere.
When my mother goes I see her coat
shining bright in the moonlight.
Her hair is black like the sky in the night.
I don't know why, but I suspect
the flower I see is my mother
that I love indeed.

Edgar Vargas, 5th grade

Here is a second example by an eighth-grade boy, Rafael, who was separated from his mother for a long period of time:

LA MADRE

La persona más dulce y comprensiva
que lo que puede ser un dulce
su mirada dulce y penetrante como
la de un águila, su corazón
fuerte y vigoroso capaz de soportar
cualquier dolor. Si yo tuviese poder
alguno buscaría en todo el universo
alguna estrella que pudiese significar
su gran amor. Cada vez que te veo en alguna foto
me recuerdo de aquellos días en que tu y yo nos
acostábamos tardísimo estudiando matemáticas,
cada vez que me veo en un espejo
se me refleja tu dulce cara y me trae una
gran sensacíon de tristeza el no poderte
tener aquí conmigo.

Rafael Angarita Matute, 8th grade

THE MOTHER

The sweetest, most understanding person,
like what a candy can be,
her sweet and penetrating glance like
that of an eagle, her heart
strong and vigorous capable of supporting
any pain. If I had any power
I would search the universe
for some star that could signify
her great love. Every time I see you in a photo
I remember the days when you and I
would go to bed so late studying math,
every time I see myself in the mirror,
your sweet face is reflected and it brings me
a great sensation of sadness to not have
you here with me.

translated by Maria Marrero

47

Sandra Calderón Charles came to New England from Spain. She had the good fortune to enter a sixth-grade class where she had two teachers fluent in Spanish. These teachers identified her gift in writing and encouraged her to write, translate, and share her extraordinary work with the school community. Many immigrant students enter schools where no one speaks their first language, in which case it is difficult, if not impossible, to discover their strengths and gifts until they acquire some fluency in English.

Sandra's poem, "Un Recuerdo," is deeply rooted in Spanish culture, in which the spirits of the deceased live on as part of the family and community. Even her grandmother's clothes have a visceral memory of the grandmother, a connection as deep as the grandchild's. The mention of the tigress and the serpent suggests female power and sexuality. This is another example of how culture permeates language development and expressive writing. Poetry is the intersection of experience and response, rational thought and intuitive emotion, family and culture:

UN RECUERDO

En el fondo de su casa vive,
su espíritu en el silencio
con sus cosas y utensilios
en la oscura eternidad.
En la ventana,
sus vestidos vuelan sin cesar,
pero no se escapan no.
Se retienen,
no se quieren ir,
su estado los detiene
parece que recuerdan a mi abuela
    alegre, tradicional,
y su boca, chiquita como una almendra,
    sus ojos, negros como la más oscura noche,
brillan sin cesar.
Con sus manos
trabajando sin cesar
trabajó contenta hasta su muerte.
Me contaron que cogió una tigresa y una serpiente.
La tigresa, amarilla como el sol con la noche
y la serpiente larga y gruesa.
Me gustaría haber estado allá, haber sido ella.
Tuvo hijos, todos fieles a su madre que fué su maestra.
Algunas veces, me arrepiento de haber nacido tan
pronto, pero no fué mi culpa.
    La vida es así: INJUSTA.

Sandra Calderón Charles, 6th grade

A MEMORY

In the back of her house lives
her spirit in silence with her belongings
in the eternal darkness.
In the window, her clothes float in the breeze
but they can't escape, no.
They are trapped,
They don't want to leave.
And it seems as though they
remember my grandmother,
 her happy traditional ways,
her mouth, small like an almond,
 her eyes, black like the darkest night
shining ceaselessly.
Her hands always working,
working contentedly until her death.
They told me that she caught a tigress and a serpent.
The tigress, yellow like the sun with the night,
and the serpent heavy and thick.
I would like to have been there, to have been her.
She had sons, all faithful to their mother, their teacher.
Sometimes I regret having been born so recently,
but the fault is not with me.
 Life is that way: UNJUST!

translated by Maria Marrero

Fifth-grader Rebecca's poem expresses ambivalence about her brother, weaving together with subtlety and grace both the irritating and the appealing aspects of their relationship:

THE PEST

He goes through my things
Like he has just found a treasure box
Finding out what is in it
For he is the brother
The pest
Teases me til I'm a volcano
Ready to blow up
For he is the brother
The teaser
Proud of the trouble he makes
Like a horse that has just won a race
Proud
For he is the brother
Like an ant forever crawling up your arm
A pain
For he is the brother

Annoying
But if you're nice
He is a kitten curled up in your arm Purring
The sweet
For he is the brother
He will sleep on the couch
Or the bed
For he is the brother
The tired one
He can be many things
The pest
The teaser
The proud
And the pain
He is the sweet
The tired one
He is many things
For he is the brother
He is the pest.

Rebecca Brager Meacham, 5th grade

When my students have access to word processing on computers at school or at home, I encourage them to enter an early draft of their poem and try several shapes and forms, options that might alter line and stanza breaks. We discuss the importance of reading the poem aloud numerous times to hear where the reader might pause or reflect on an image. Line breaks and form in free verse are difficult concepts because there are few rules to guide the writer. Ideally, teachers will show their students a wide range of poetry on the page so that the connection between form and meaning begins to be recognized by students as they proceed through the grades.

Word processing allowed Rebecca to try many versions of her poem, several left-justified, and this one, centered. Ultimately, the writer must choose a visual form based on personal style and taste.

The following poems emerged from extensive discussions about what objects, rituals, talents, stories, songs, personality traits, and names have been passed down through family generations and reflect something about the family's roots, culture, or values. In the next poem, sixth-grader Nicole examines the feeling of receiving an heirloom and articulates how she is a link in her continuing family history:

HERITAGE, A RING FROM PERU

The feeling, the wonder
whose hands chiseled that
intricate design on the gold,
The sheen and sparkle with

every movement, as if alive,
like a part of me.
I am the second receiver,
as it slowly turns into a long
spiral of remembrance,
a gift received again and again.
Still, a feeling of pride
with each bestowing.
I was the receiver and I
will be the giver.

Nicole Shalhoub, 6th grade

Elona came to the United States from Russia as a young child. Her poem, written when she was in the fifth grade, addresses the photo album that can speak and tell secrets of the family's history. The album displays the range of family fortunes through symbol and metaphor:

ALBUM

The brown snakeskin album,
rather new, unlike
the pictures inside.
I ask him,
what story do you
have to tell?
And he replies,
I have the story
of sun and sand.
Of bricks in gold
and bricks in lead.
Of friend and family.
I am a long precious
ribbon of history
and life.

Elona Prilutsky, 5th grade

In reflecting on her family name, seventh-grader Chandra has borrowed from the form and mystery of Emily Dickinson. The poem breaks out of this form the way an adolescent would pull away from her family to establish her own independence and voice:

THERE IS NO SECRET

There is no secret to my name,
No myth that I should hide,
There is no password or code,
It's not as solid as ice,

It doesn't drift upon the wind,
Or float the sea with ease,
There is no rhyme or reason,
no melody to sing.

It does not give me special power,
Nor does it weaken me,
It does not label or have much meaning,
It's really not a thing.

My name is here like a shadow,
To give me a blanket of existence,
Shelter me,
Feed me,
Clothe me,

I do not complain.
Boo or hiss like the rain,
But smile like steel
To show the me inside the beast,
Proud I'll be of my name.

Chandra Edwards, 7th grade

On the original draft, I indicated to Chandra where she had left the form behind and suggested that she reconsider the diction and image in two circled phrases. She rejected my recommendation in two successive conferences in favor of her original language.

In describing one of the ways in which poetry differs from prose for her, Chandra said, "Poetry is a fine activity and it can get you in tune with yourself, more than a book [of fiction] might. A book, you're writing basically for somebody. With poetry you're writing what comes from the soul and is meant for yourself — unless you want to share it."

Reflecting on this sampling of family poems, I see that some cultures respect family members so highly that children from those cultures do not usually consider including ambivalent feelings in a piece of writing. In contrast, other cultures encourage children to feel and even express their ambivalence. Culture also influences the subject matter, the writer's response, the central images, the diction, and the cadence chosen by each child for his or her poem. While poems provide a small manageable form, they invite the child's whole life and language experience inside. Children feel and write passionately about their families, feel deeply invested in poems that derive from family sources, and have a keen interest in the family lives of classmates as expressed in their poems. Reading poems such as these in front of a class requires courage and trust. Children are usually respectful and sometimes even awed by what they learn about and connect to in their classmates' poetry. Through the poems read and written in classrooms, I am allowed entry into children's spiritual lives, their closest relationships, their powerful ambivalences — in other words, into the core that drives their thinking and development.

We must surround our students with poetry, and this poetry must represent our pluralistic society and even the diversity of languages our children speak at home. It is not unusual to walk into an urban classroom and find four or five new students who speak no English. I have had to find poems in many languages so that these children can be a part of our exploration of literature. As students learn English, they often excel in writing poetry because they pay attention to every word and construction, each sound, and the various connotations of meaning. Poetry is also less confining than prose with regard to grammatical structure.

Beginning in the 1960s, a growing number of publishers has allowed and encouraged access to publishing by women and people of color. Our students have a chance to *be* writers and *to be heard,* which was not true before. Now we have an even greater obligation to bring diverse literature to our students. Peggy McIntosh, codirector of Wellesley College's Center for Research on Women, urges us to provide "mirrors and windows": "mirrors" to see writers who reflect ourselves and "windows" to see what writers of other cultures offer us.

Encouraging children to write their own poems is not meant to turn them all into poets, any more than teaching the writing process is meant to transform all children into novelists or essayists. Although a few students will go on to be successful writers, many more will simply feel comfortable expressing themselves in a variety of forms or genres for their own delight or work. Most students will take a deeper pleasure in classic and contemporary literature, enriching their intellectual, imaginative, and emotional lives. Reading poetry, understanding a poem, recognizing your life in it, taking it to heart, and writing your own life into the world's new literature is a humanizing, compassionate, intellectual, and breathtaking endeavor.

IT AND I

Does it walk in the field with you?
  yes, yes,
Does it whisper and wish with you?
It walks ahead of me when I walk
and the wind whirls the words for it.

Sarah Larysz, 3rd grade

The Uses of Folk Music and Songwriting in the Classroom

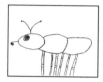

VICTOR COCKBURN

Folk music and song have always fascinated me. As a child of West Indian parents, I sensed the importance of music in the Calypso songs that my parents played on records and sang from memory. I remember that the songs dealt with everything from political statements to lullabies with joyful enthusiasm and spontaneous improvisation.

The power of folk music as a means of individual expression and social change became even more evident to me as a teenager when I attended a concert at the Brooklyn Academy of Music. Performed by folk singer and social activist Pete Seeger, folk singer Odetta, and the Reverend Gary Davis, a Gospel-blues singer, recording artist, and minister, the concert was my first exposure to folk music as a tool for social change. The simple beauty of the music and power of the lyrics inspired me to become more deeply involved with this universal form of expression. The effect it had on the audience — bringing a large roomful of people together in song — and the information and history I learned through the music motivated me to learn more about folk music. That event inspired me to learn how to play the guitar and explore folk music and song, initially through the composition of others and eventually through my own.

My educational experience between 1968 and 1972 had a profound effect on my philosophy and on my continuing exploration of creative self-expression as a teaching and learning tool. I spent those years as a student in the Friends World College (FWC), an experimental college based on pioneer educator Morris Mitchell's philosophy of global, experiential education. Each student's curriculum was formulated by the student and a faculty advisor. After an orientation semester at the North American campus in Huntington, New York, the students lived and studied at the college's campuses

Harvard Educational Review Vol. 61 No. 1 February 1991

in Africa, Mexico, England, and other countries over the next four years. I had the fortune to study ethnomusicology in several countries during my years at FWC and was deeply affected by the central role music — particularly folk music and song — played in various cultures.

When I returned to the United States in 1972 from my studies in Mexico, England, Ireland, and the East African countries of Kenya, Uganda, and Tanzania, I became an artist-educator. I was introduced to the possibility of combining my skills as a songwriter, my educational experience, and my interest in the educational development of children through a collective of artists living in Cambridge, Massachusetts, now known as Cooperative Artists Institute.

This small, dedicated group of talented and ethnically diverse artists collectively managed their nonprofit educational organization. These musicians, dancers, visual artists, and writers were beginning to explore ways of developing a more meaningful relationship between the artist and the educator. As I lived and worked closely with this group, I soon recognized the importance of combining the art of folk music with classroom curriculum, of using creative expression as a tool for teaching and learning.

In 1974 I launched my own program, "Folkshop," taking into classrooms my skills as a songwriter and folk singer, as well as my experience in blending educational techniques with my art form. Thanks to the generosity and guidance of teachers in the Brookline and Newton school systems in Massachusetts, I was able to present in-class workshops at different grade levels. I began to compose songs with the students that were based on curriculum topics and areas of interest to the class — such as history, social studies, science, and nature — using traditional melodies and writing techniques appropriate to each grade level. Through songwriting, I could blend techniques of reading and writing with the process of creative expression in an art form that was already familiar — even to kindergartners.

The Function of Folk Song in the Classroom

Folk music has always involved the passing on of information: from nation to nation, generation to generation, culture to culture; between man and woman, parent and child, child and child. Folk music is the music and songs of ordinary people, passed on in the oral tradition. A lullaby sung by a mother to a baby, a jump-rope chant passed from fifth graders to third graders on a school playground, field and ship worker songs, and hymns passed on from elders to youth in places of worship are some examples of how songs communicate across generations and cultural boundaries. In *The Book of Music* (1978), editor Gil Rowley comments:

Victor Cockburn sings along with children in a bilingual kindergarten class at the Mattahunt School in Mattapan, Massachusetts.

> Three more factors help give folk song its final shape. They are continuity (many performances over a number of years); variation (changes in words and melodies either through artistic interpretation or failure of memory); and selection (the acceptance of a song or tune by the community in which it evolves). (p. 68)

Folk songs have always been an excellent vehicle for storytelling and teaching. Some older ballads, sea shanties, and western songs have numerous verses that relate entire stories and offer experiences and observations about life. Folk songs are intended for off-key singers, amateur musicians, whistlers, hand clappers, and folks who love a good song enough to want to join in. Songs of the Labor Movement, for example, have the greatest impact if those singing can *hear* the words of struggle and *feel* the bond they form among workers of different cultural backgrounds, the feeling that comes from many voices rising together. A folk song written by students in a classroom has value to its own community because of the shared effort in its creation and the familiarity of the subject matter to others in the community.

The Artist-Teacher Partnership

Over the years I have come to appreciate and respect the importance of the artist-teacher partnership. Most of my successful artist-in-residence programs begin with an in-service workshop for teachers and staff in which I demonstrate the techniques I use in the classroom and involve the teachers in the creative process of folk-song writing. The workshop helps establish the artist-teacher partnership, an alliance that is important if the teacher is to continue to feel comfortable using songwriting techniques after I have left the classroom.

When the teacher is an enthusiastic participant, it supports the children's inspiration and enthusiasm and the teacher's confidence in attempting to write a group song again. In the classroom, the teacher is the role model for creative risk-taking. The teacher who can comfortably integrate an interest in music, literature, and art into a teaching style and classroom curriculum demonstrates how integral art and creative expression are in our everyday lives. This integration also helps the students feel that songwriting is related to their learning and can inspire in them an interest in these subjects.

Interaction plays an important role in folk music, and I advise teachers to participate actively. You don't have to know how to read music or sing like a well-trained vocalist; the idea is to sing together, even if you sing along with a tape recorder or record player. Over the years I have encountered many teachers who have been inspired to use folk song and songwriting in their teaching. These teachers are usually people who are enough at ease with their students to feel "safe" singing in front of them.

Some teachers, however, are uncomfortable with the idea of singing with their classes; sometimes, when students and I are sitting together, singing and swapping songs, the teacher leaves. It is difficult for a guest artist to proceed when the teacher is absent from the class, and it is also disheartening to realize that the teacher is not likely to use my techniques when I have left the classroom. Without establishing some partnership with the teacher, my program becomes mere entertainment and loses its "soul," its educational core — the use of creative expression in the form of folk song as support for language arts and other areas of study.

It is these very teachers, however, that I am most interested in trying to help. Within the setting of a teacher in-service workshop and in the company of peers, an otherwise self-conscious teacher might be caught up in the joy and group dynamics of singing a folk song. If, with my support, the teacher can carry this feeling into the classroom, then there is a chance my program will continue after I leave the school. My hope is to inspire in teachers and students the confidence and ability to sing together and to connect songwriting to their studies and to other matters of importance. I also hope to help them create the atmosphere necessary for creative expression, an environment in which folk song can cross cultural barriers and promote a deeper understanding of universal themes. Because writing songs is part of the oral process and can be employed by teachers who are not trained in music, I never write any musical notes on the board. If a class wishes to notate a song, I encourage them to invite their music specialist in for help.

I have also returned to schools where teachers with whom I have worked continue to use songwriting with tremendous enthusiasm. The following is a song that one such teacher wrote with her second-grade class. It demonstrates the writing technique of comparison (simile), while complementing the curriculum unit on ocean life:

THE GREAT OCEAN

The ocean is like a mirror,
It reflects the light blue sky.
When the wind blows like an angry storm,
It lifts the waves so high.

When they land they splash,
It all looks so grand.
Rocks, seaweed, coral,
Shells, water, sand.

The Classroom Workshops

During the first session of a typical three-session residency, I introduce both traditional and contemporary songs appropriate to the grade level. I give examples of how the medium conveys both historical data and commonsense wisdom, and I always include songs in other languages to demonstrate the universality of lyrical expression and thematic material. Depending on the theme a teacher selects, such as westward expansion, freedom and slavery, war and peace, or the Industrial Revolution, I bring in relevant songs and ask students to listen for the various forms of expression and divergent points of view. I encourage participation in singing as well as in discussing the source of material and lyrical style.

A series of songs on westward expansion, for example, might trace the journeys of American pioneers from their European roots through their hardships and explorations as they crossed the North American continent. The lyrical images in the songs of Native American tribes relate to nature, the environment, myths, and legends. Songs of the African-American culture reflect distinct musical styles from West Africa, blended with musical styles from Latin America, and speak of the struggle against slavery. Some elements of all of these strands have merged into a new global folk music, currently called "world beat."

At the end of the first session I give the class an assignment to collect folk songs from their homes. The songs must be passed down in the oral tradition, not copied from record or tape jackets or songbooks; the students must write them down or tape-record them. The assignment includes conducting a short interview with the person from whom the song was learned. Students whose families speak another language at home are encouraged to collect songs in their native language, and to include a translation if possible.

At the beginning of the second session, these songs are shared. On many occasions, students (and some teachers) have brought in original songs composed by parents or grandparents, variations of those songs, or versions of songs that were learned by their parents at an early age. This classroom collection is respected and treated as unique; it demonstrates both the diversity of folk music and the cross-cultural links we share.

During the second session we begin to write lyrics for a group song based on either the curriculum unit or an area of interest to the class, such as homework, recess, health, or safety. As preparation for songwriting, I advise teachers to bring in records, either from home or from the library, and to photocopy the lyrics so the students can follow the words and identify the written structure of the song. Writing the lyrics of a group song on the blackboard solves the problems encountered when writing individually: How do I start? What do I want to say? What form shall I use? The melody is secondary to the composition of the lyrics because, as we shall see, melody can be adapted to the lyrical structure.

While there are many forms and rhyme schemes for song lyrics, I encourage using the ballad form. In the Teachers and Writers Collaborative's *The Handbook of Poetic Forms* (1987), ballad is described as "a popular poetic form [used] all over the world. People make up and sing ballads in cultures that have no reading or writing, as well as in those that do" (p. 17). The ballad was derived from folk song and has a long history as a medium for expressing opinion and conveying information. I recommend using a simple rhyme scheme for the verses, such as ABCB, in which only the second and the fourth lines rhyme, so that rhyming does not overshadow the lyrical content.

Topic Selection

I usually recommend that topics be narrowed to a particular focus: for example, it may be better to focus on one favorite sport, such as baseball, than to write a song about sports in general. A closer look will turn up interesting details, such as the "crack" sound the ball makes on contact with the bat, or the roar and tension of a good crowd of fans, or the smell of the popcorn and hot dogs. Incorporating sensory images enriches the lyrics of a song and often provides a good starting point.

I begin by soliciting suggestions from the children for possible lines. An idea for a line should bounce around the room like a balloon; an idea offered by one child in a group is then honed by another. I encourage the children to listen carefully to each other for good ideas and suggestions. Everyone, even shy children, gets caught up in the thrill of creating a new song.

The song "Shells," by a second-grade class at the Plympton School in Waltham, Massachusetts, illustrates how information and feeling is conveyed through the lyrics of a song. Impressions and observations of a study trip to the ocean are recalled and shared, and the words are put to the tune of "When Irish Eyes Are Smiling" (Too Ra Loo Ra Loo Ra). The children were encouraged to describe their sense of the environment and their role in it. They were also asked to use academic facts and observational impressions, as well as figurative language, to convey information about different seaside creatures. The end result is a song with memorable facts and images, a familiar tune, and a repeating chorus that enabled others to join in and sing.

SHELLS
(to the tune of "When Irish Eyes Are Smiling")

Sea shells by the rocks in the tidepools by the ocean.
Many colors, different sizes, all around me by the sea.
The ocean waves lapping, sounded like hands clapping.
The sky was cloudy, the seagulls spoke to me.

Blue mussels, barnacles, clams, and quahogs	(A)
Scallops, jingle shells, and angel wings	(B)
Under rocks all around us, a real pretty sight	(C)
To the periwinkle, we did sing	(D)

Sea shells by the rocks in the tidepools by the ocean.
Many colors, different sizes, all around me by the sea.
The ocean waves lapping, sounded like hands clapping.
The sky was cloudy, the seagulls spoke to me.

Bi-valves have two shells that open with hinges,	(A)
Scallops look like Spanish abanicos with fringes.	(A)
Moon snails close their operculum tight	(B)
When the tide goes out or when you give them a fright.	(B)

Second Grade, Plympton School, Waltham, Massachusetts

In another example, a kindergarten class in Brookline was exploring ocean life, and dolphins in particular. Using the information that the children had gained through classroom discussion and study and combining two tunes familiar to this age group ("Skip to My Lou" and "This Land Is Your Land"), the children used their own words to describe their knowledge and feelings about these animals.

I asked the children to tell me where the dolphins lived (line number one), and to describe the ocean (line number two). In line number three, they identified with the dolphin (everyone has friends), and the last line (the key rhyme) described dolphin's playful personalities. The rhyme form again was ABCB, and we repeated it for the next eight lines. I let the rhyme be subordinate to the content, rather than the reverse. For this age group, rhymes can be kept to one per stanza until everyone gets the idea, and then they can experiment with more complex patterns.

When we finished the third verse, the children suggested a refrain. This was not unusual, since most of the songs I sang with them had one. A boy started a joyful chant, "I wanna be a dolphin, I wanna be a dolphin." The song, "This Land Is Your Land," seemed a natural for all of us, and the fact of combining the songs did not bother a soul. The entire class felt that they had contributed to the development of a new song, and they were easily able to follow the written words on the blackboard. Their words:

DOLPHINS
(to the tune of "Skip to My Lou")

The dolphin lives in the ocean,
The wavy wavy sea.
The dolphin has many friends,
And they're as cute as can be.

The dolphin took a dive in
The wavy, wavy sea.
His blue body flashing like lightning,
Looked so pretty to me.

The dolphin has many enemies,
Like the shark and the killer whale.
The dolphin swims away from them,
By using his powerful tail.

And I want to be a dolphin
I want to be a dolphin
Swimming in the wavy,
Wavy sea.

I want to be a dolphin,
I want to be a dolphin,
Splashing in the water
Just you and me.

Kindergarten, Driscoll School, Brookline, Massachusetts

The children had followed the same process I use in writing a song. I ask myself questions about what information or feeling I am trying to convey. I have many ideas, and I have to decide which "path" I want the song to take. I look for descriptive words and comparative phrases to convey clearly what I wish to say.

Once the lyrics were written on the board, we sang the song through several times, adapting the melody to the lyrics. I let the melody of the original tune shift with the different syllables' cadence, sometimes slowly drawing out, sometimes moving more quickly along. For example, the first line of the dolphin song, with eight instead of six syllables, does not fit exactly to the tune of "Skip, skip, skip to my Lou," so we altered the phrasing a bit.

When working on a song with a class, I might ask a student or teacher to try singing the song *a capella* in his or her own natural key. We might then play with the rhythms. The original tune may go through several permutations in a matter of minutes, but the song will, in time, settle into a consistent melody.

Another approach to putting music to the words is "tune doodling." The first and perhaps most obvious way is to use a standard tune, as I have already discussed. This method requires a compromise between the syllables of the lyrics and the meter of the selected melody in the quickening or elongation of the words to suit the rhythm or the melody. There are more restrictions with this method, and one may have to try several different melodies to effect a marriageable mix.

The second way is to create a melody of your own. Tune doodling, as in drawing-doodling, requires a "letting go" — a relaxing of the mind enough to allow an intuitive melody to rise to the surface and be vocalized, to be woven around the lyrics. The results are often bits and pieces of remembered melodies strung along in serendipity. When I ask children to try this, I start by asking them to read the words of a verse through slowly, paying attention to the rhythm and cadence of the words. Sometimes this has to be repeated until they feel comfortable with the words. I then proceed from reading to chanting, and then on to singing. When this is done, I ask the students to give each word a note and to read it through "singingly." In nearly all cases, the last word of the last line is musically resolved, regardless of how disjointedly the other lines were sung — a phenomenon stemming from our experiences and expectations of what a song is. I then build on the invented melody, and, with some repetition, the tune becomes established.

Pete Seeger said, "It's not the singer or the song, but the singer, the song, and the situation": the choice of melody and how it is delivered can determine whether a song will make you laugh or cry. I ask children to give the song respect from the start — if it's funny, sing it so, and if it's serious, set the mood for listening. I tell them that if they always enjoy singing it, so will others.

Bilingual Songs

Many classrooms today are composed of students from a mosaic of cultures. By exposing students to a wide variety of global folk music and songs and by combining languages and melodies from different cultures, the common thread of expression takes on another dimension. In the bilingual classroom, songwriting has the expanded function of helping students learn each other's languages and cultures. The following are two examples of this method, the first in Spanish and English, the second in Hebrew and English.

> ES LINDA LA NIEVE (The Snow Is Pretty)
>
> Winter is cold as a freezer,
> I feel like I am made of ice.
> I slip when I walk on the sidewalk,
> My coat feels warm and nice.
>
> Es linda la nieve. The snow is pretty.
> Cuando cae la primera vez. When it falls for the first time.
> (repeat)
>
> I like to play in the snow,
> I make buildings and throw snowballs.
> I play outside with my friends,
> When they come to call.
>
> Es linda la nieve,
> Cuando cae la primera vez.
> (repeat)
>
> *First grade, Lehey School, Lawrence, Massachusetts*

"Es Linda la Nieve" was written in a predominantly Spanish-speaking school in Lawrence, Massachusetts. The chorus of the song is in Spanish and reflects the lyrical content of the verses. The melody was invented — or "doodled" — by a student in the class and is Latin in rhythm and melody.

Creating songs like this values a child's first language while he or she learns a new one and gives everyone the pleasure of using words from two languages. The universal love for singing is a great motivation for reading and understanding new words.

Recently I was invited to be Artist-in-Residence at a traditional Hebrew school. I was the first artist they had invited to work with the teachers and students for a significant length of time. I had to pay particular attention to religious beliefs and customs, and it took me several weeks to discover that melodies in minor keys, recalling traditional Yiddish and Hebrew songs, made students and teachers feel more at home with my program. I studied the songs of the culture and eventually wrote bilingual songs with some of the classes.

LIVING TOGETHER IN PEACE

Living together in peace,
Peace is in our home.
Living together in peace,
Chaim byachad beshalom.
(He 'eem be a kad bi shalom)
Love is sharing with friends,
Be caring everyday.
Sharing what you have,
Ohave velo sonay.
(Oheav villo sonay)

3A and 3B, Maimonides School, Brookline, Massachusetts

"Living Together in Peace," written in the Hebrew school, weaves both Hebrew and English into the verse so that they rhyme with one another. The melody in the minor key appropriate to Hebrew culture was also invented by a student.

Conclusion

I believe that folk song in the classroom is a valuable and accessible tool for the teacher who is not trained in music. In the classroom environment, the great variety of available recorded material and resources can enhance almost all curriculum units in some way. Writing folk songs is an effective tool for teaching language arts, for developing skills of observation and problem-solving, and for inspiring confidence in creative expression. The universality of folk song can also be used to develop an understanding of and appreciation for a variety of cultures, and as an aid in bilingual education.

In my role as a visiting artist, I have sung with thousands of students and teachers, visited hundreds of classrooms, and written an almost equal number of songs in a wide variety of schools. Like many of the songs written and sung by the common folk throughout the world, not all of these songs survive. Some, however, will, and they will be passed along. They may be changed — lyrics added, melody reused, perhaps the original authors forgotten — and some may become "traditional" over time.

Through the writing and sharing of new songs, we help to keep alive the folk process and affirm the continuation of knowledge and experience.

> Alas for those who never sing,
> But die with all their music in them.
>
> *Oliver Wendell Holmes*

References

Padgett, R. (Ed.). (1987). *The handbook of poetic forms.* New York: Teachers and Writers Collaborative.

Rowley, G. (1978). *The book of music.* Englewood Cliffs, NJ: Prentice-Hall.

Tribal Rhythms®: A Thematic Approach to Integrating the Arts into the Curriculum

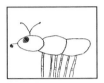

BARBARA BECKWITH
W. THOMPSON GARFIELD
CHARLES M. HOLLEY
J. CURTIS JONES
SUSAN E. PORTER

Tribal Rhythms, an interdisciplinary arts program of Cooperative Artists Institute, acts as an educational strategy to help schools deal with urgent problems facing today's children, including family fragmentation, loss of community, social and racial isolation, low self-esteem, and deteriorating academic achievement.

All of us in our Tribal Rhythms foursome are professional artists; two of us have been classroom teachers with psychology and education degrees. An important feature of the group is that we are interracial: Charles and Curtis are African-American; Tom and Susan are European-American. The value of this diversity is that the children see adults of different races working together in a positive way. We believe the program is powerful and effective because it incorporates our various cultural perspectives, experiences, and artistic expertise.

Over the last twenty years. Tribal Rhythms has run one-time programs in close to one thousand Massachusetts public and private schools, three- to ten-session short-term programs in seventy-five schools, and long-term in-depth programs lasting from one to three years in over thirty-five elementary or middle schools.

Harvard Educational Review   Vol. 61   No. 3   August 1991

Our goal is to help educators create socially inclusive learning environments in which each person is respected; in which leadership, initiative, and innovation are encouraged; and in which each student achieves academic excellence. Such a learning environment uses a variety of teaching approaches that match the children's diverse learning styles and reflects the cultures and interests of students and teachers. Most importantly, this environment brings out the playful, creative person in both teacher and student, and gives them effective problem-solving skills.

In Tribal Rhythms, the theme of "tribe" serves as a powerful model for an ideal learning environment. Historically, if you trace back far enough into every person's ancestry, you'll find there is a tribe. In the context of our program, we define "tribe" as a community, extended family, or any group of people with shared values, experiences, and identity. Because the theme of "tribe" satisfies a powerful human need for connectedness, belonging, and trust, it allows us to create a socially inclusive learning environment. The tribal theme ties together history, science and technology, social studies, language, and physical and social development, putting the entire curriculum into a real-life context. It gives teachers a framework in which cooperative learning, community spirit, democratic values, self-esteem, and multicultural understanding can thrive.

Our second theme is "the artist in self." We believe that everyone has inherent creative abilities. Bringing out the artistic self helps the person meet a basic human need for self-expression. The process of creating art can change people's behavior and transform their lives. The arts can be a "tool" for shaping a new reality, and can transform social groups, heal tensions, and build a sense of community.

* * *

Music fills the echoey room as the 150 third, fourth, and fifth graders, their teachers, and their principal file into the gym at Beeman Memorial School in Gloucester, Massachusetts.

Charley is beating a resonant, regular, soothing rhythm on a handmade log drum. The rest of us join in with handmade instruments: a tin-can bell, a bamboo flute, a dried-gourd rattle. Behind us, the Tribal Rhythms banner reads: "There was a person who made a circle to keep me out so I made a circle to include us both."

The teachers arrange their classes in neat semicircular rows, then settle into folding chairs at the rear, like sentinels. One teacher sips coffee, another corrects papers, a third conscientiously scans the crowd for signs of disruption. The children, seated crosslegged on the floor, are mesmerized by the variety of handmade musical instruments we are playing.

Teachers and students at the Bowman School, Lexington, Massachusetts, join in the Tribal Yell.

As the music continues, Susan begins the Tribal Rhythms performance by talking about the idea of tribe. "If you go back far enough in your family," she says, "no matter how different we look, speak, or act, we ALL come from tribes. A tribe is a group of people who are like a family or a community. And what makes a 'together' tribe?" The children raise their hands, some wiggling their fingers with eagerness. Susan collects all their ideas. In a together tribe, they say, everyone cooperates, shares ideas, respects everyone else in the tribe, and cares about each other.

"In these ways, the Beeman School is like a tribe, and today we're here to celebrate YOUR tribe," says Susan. She then shows them the Tribal Sign. The youngsters learn to make two circles with thumb and index finger, link those circles paper-chain style, and hold them high in the air — the sign for respectful silence. To try it out, she gets everyone gabbing noisily and making sounds. At the Tribal Sign, they STOP. Ragged results — we try again. This time, everyone stops at the same moment, and the roomful of children burst out with satisfied laughter. They've done something together and it worked. The teachers laugh too. Four teachers join in on the first try. On the second try, another teacher looks sideways to check that others have joined in, then raises his arms as well to make the sign.

Now the Tribal Yell. Susan explains that this is a way for us to hear how powerful a group can be when they're really together — when they know how to cooperate. She leads the children in slapping their thighs along with a rhythmic drum beat from Charley. On the count of three, everyone raises their arms to give voice to a thunderous yell. Then down come their arms — and the noise turns to silence.

Now Tom takes the center stage and the rest of us continue the music in the background. "An important part of today's celebration is the arts," says Tom. "There's an artist in all of us. In you, too. But you already knew that, right?" Some children call out "yes," but others shake their heads "no."

"Yes, in you, too," says Tom. "Whenever you dance or paint or even cook an incredible meal — anything that you do the best you can do and use your imagination, your creativity for, is art. We're going to start with music. What is music anyway?"

A flurry of hands go up. "Sounds that go together," one child offers. "Yes, and sounds that express feelings, too," says Tom. "What do people use to make music? People around the world make music from whatever they have around," he says, holding out a drum made from a steel mixing bowl. He explains how it's made, while Curtis mimes stretching the animal hide over a log drum from Haiti. Charley begins a mesmerizing drum rhythm. Susan plays a trill on a Japanese flute carved from bamboo. Curtis plays a cowbell from India, and Tom joins in the music by scratching a stick against a cheese grater. "Even your fingers can make music," says Tom, snapping his fingers, "and your voice is an instrument too." He breaks into a silly "la la, la la" song and the children join in, making sounds together. Laughter — an important ingredient of the Tribal Rhythms Program — fills the room.

Now Charley involves the whole audience in the story of how we imagine music might have begun. He sets the scene and transports the entire audience to a time long ago, as Curtis, Susan, and Tom dramatize the action of the story:

> Long ago people had no way to get warm, and they were so cold (we shiver). Finally, these people from long ago discover fire (we warm our rear-ends by a fire — the children laugh). Now the people are clothed and fed, but still they're unhappy because they're bored. One day, out of frustration, one person bangs two rocks together in rhythm (Curtis hits the drum). The others like it and join in with hand-clapping and voices. Soon everyone is making music.

Susan pulls instruments from a bag, one for each child and adult in the room. At first, the kids look anxious — "I want one, me, me!" — but there's enough for all. The teacher who was correcting papers puts them down —

she needs two hands to play a "guirro" scraper — a length of bamboo with ridges for scraping with a stick.

Charley leads the music-making. Every kid and teacher joins in. We use a bell and vocals to weave a thread around the room that pulls all the sounds into one tune. As the children find the tune, they play in sync with each other. Children swap their instruments to try out each other's sounds. It's like a chemical change: they've jelled as a group. The intensity grows. Then with a sweep of his arms, Charley brings the music to a halt. "That was great. We knew there were a lot of musicians in this group." The audience is a sea of smiling faces.

The spell is broken when Charley shouts: "Where is Curtis?" Children and teachers look around. Curtis is missing. He then comes running back, but he's scared — he has seen a mysterious creature! He can't think of words to describe it, so he tries to show it. Curtis asks Susan to help. One by one, he invites children to form a line behind her. The serpentine line grows to include all the children and teachers, and the principal as well. Then Charley begins a rhythm on the drum, and the "creature" begins weaving around the gym. Now Curtis moves his hips in rhythm, waves his hands over his head, and directs everyone to follow.

After a series of animated movements, the dance ends with a collective "SSHHsshh," and everyone settles back to the floor. Tom congratulates everyone for creating a successful celebration together. "Just as we all helped Curtis describe the mysterious creature he saw by dancing," he says, "the artist in us all can communicate what we see and feel. If we don't have a word for something, we can use sculpture, dance, music, storytelling — all of the arts to express ourselves."

There's time for students' questions and reactions: "How'd you get the idea of Tribal Rhythms?" "How'd you make the instruments?" "How old are you?" "Would you play at my birthday party?" "How did you get together?" And, "That was fun!"

Fun — yes. But that's not all that was going on. Tribal Rhythms is more than entertainment. The program draws people in, step by step, to create a temporary culture that transforms even the most varied groups of people into a single "tribe." We use the arts to solve real problems. At each school, we collaborate with the teachers to work on the problems they see: from fighting and name-calling, to academic problems and inattention to teachers, to low self-esteem and racial or ethnic polarization.

Our performances use concrete techniques: fun, repetitive activities that channel energy into group activity and then back to calm. Teachers often worry that vigorous, expressive group activity will lead to chaos, but we know that out of the process of group-building, responsibility to others emerges naturally. Activities such as the Tribal Yell, Tribal Sign, and Tribal Sigh give youngsters a vehicle for using their bodies and voices to build group identity, rather than to disrupt it. These techniques make discipline something they want to do. We call this "dynamic control."

The Tribal Sign works, for instance, because it's an active way to achieve silence. When we use the Tribal Sign, peer pressure does the rest: the kids remind each other to be quiet. And the Tribal Sigh "brings kids down" from vigorous activity to peaceful silence with slow expulsion of breath that calms bodies and minds.

An introductory Tribal Rhythms performance may lead to a program lasting from several months to several years. In the longer-term projects, we meet regularly with teachers to develop activities that address their concerns and meet their objectives. After each session, we give teachers follow-up arts activities along with academic and discussion topics to use the very next day. Tribal Rhythms may be at a school for an hour, a day, a month, or a year. When we leave, teachers have the tools to continue using program themes, techniques, and activities in their classrooms.

In 1986, the Harvard-Kent School in Charlestown, Massachusetts, asked Tribal Rhythms to help integrate members of the Cluster Program (for abused and emotionally disturbed children) and Asian-bilingual students with the rest of the school to help create a more cohesive community. The 650 K–5 students who attend the school are primarily Chinese, Cambodian, Hispanic, and African-American. They travel from various neighborhoods across the city to attend the school.

Before our program came to the school, children from Harvard-Kent's different programs rarely met each other or even learned each other's names. On the playground, they often fought or poked fun at each other. The teachers and the principal had said that they were concerned about the isolation of the bilingual and special-needs students, who rarely interacted with the rest of the school.

Our goal was to help the school create common experiences that would build a sense of connectedness. We wanted the whole school to see itself in a new way, as a joint "we," while respecting each other's individual and ethnic differences. We wanted the children and teachers to see that everyone in the school had something to contribute, and that each group of students was an important part of the whole. Once the school felt "together" as a community, we knew they would be able to get on with the business of teaching and learning.

To achieve these goals, over a two-year period we created a combination of teacher and student workshops and performances that would build a strong sense of community in the school. Every student in the school met with us for activities at least once a month, and many students met with us more often. The teachers met with us for in-service workshops every other

Student and teachers at the Bowman school join in the "dance of the mysterious creature."

month, since with all our performances and workshops we always provide teachers with preparation and follow-up activity ideas to reinforce the academic and social skills each activity focused on.

We started with our usual introductory performance to establish the new theme of tribe and community, and continued with a series of activities chosen to reinforce this theme. For example, we involved students in acting out "The Story of the Weakest and Strongest," a tale about a tribe that discovers the meaning of respect. In this performance, students switch roles throughout so they get a chance to act out the roles of both the Weakest (the underdog) and the Strongest (the bully). The story takes place in pre-verbal history and involves a tribe that is "untogether." The story unfolds like this:

> No one gets along with each other. The Weakest is harassed by the Strongest, and everyone else joins in. At first, the whole tribe ridicules the Weakest. The ridicule goes on, and makes everyone miserable. No one is having fun or getting much done. The tribe is trapped by its own negative behavior but doesn't know a way out.
>
> At one point in the story, the Weakest is crying and wailing, when suddenly, a spark of creativity inspires him. Something in the sounds he is

making pleases him. He begins to weave the sounds into a melodious song. Others slowly join in.

The Strongest tries to stop them and has a temper tantrum, but for the first time they're all together, they're having fun and they're not going to let him ruin their good time. When he realizes he can no longer make the group do what he wants, he joins in himself. Finally, everyone can see that even the Weakest member has something to contribute to the whole group.

When the untogether tribe finally gets together, there's a release of tension and a mutual sense of happiness that makes everyone enjoy and appreciate each other. Everyone celebrates the togetherness of the tribe — and the specialness of each person in it.

After experiencing the story of "The Weakest and the Strongest," the kids were able to talk about how, when they label someone "the new kid," or "skinny," or "a foreigner," they don't see what that person has to offer. The Harvard-Kent teachers found in the weeks following that when a situation of intimidation started to erupt, the children would say, "You're acting like the guy in the story of the bully." Their shared experience helped diffuse conflict much better than if the teacher had simply set a "don't shove, don't tease" rule.

The teachers also commented that the students were able to see "bullies" in a new way — that bullies rarely have real friends, and people fear but don't like them. The kids who had bossed others around started thinking that they didn't want to be bullies. And kids who felt like "outsiders" started to see themselves as having hidden gifts and talents and a role in the group.

In order to create new relationships between children in the different groups, we combined students from the Asian-bilingual classes, the special-needs Cluster Program, and the rest of the school to do a series of activities together. These included instrument- and jewelry-making, and dance and acting workshops. In the process, both teachers and students got to know people from the other groups very well over time.

At first, classes stayed very separate; the teachers and students sat with their own groups. In the later sessions, however, the teachers sat together and jointly supervised the entire group, and then the students began to mingle.

One first grader, who had used ethnic slurs against the Asian students in the past, became comfortable enough after playing instruments and acting out dramatic stories together with Asian students and teachers to go to a Chinese teacher for cuddling and hugs as the program progressed.

In addition to addressing the problem of isolation of the students in the Cluster Program, we also created activities to help their teachers with the students' other therapeutic needs. These students suffered from a range of serious emotional, behavioral, and learning problems that prevented them from being able to learn in a regular classroom environment. In collaboration with the Cluster Program staff, we determined that project activities should focus on building the students' self-esteem. We developed activities that were interesting, safe, and engaging, and that guaranteed the students' success. Students who were often disruptive or emotionally withdrawn began to get involved without losing interest or acting out. Teachers and the school psychologist reported that the children showed increased self-confidence and a real feeling of accomplishment.

In a series of banner-making sessions, we planned activities so that students in the Cluster Program would have to work in groups to design and construct large banners depicting themes of friendship, cooperation, and respect. The banners were to be displayed throughout the school as a gift from the Cluster Program students to the entire school community.

Assisted by teachers and the Tribal Rhythms artists, the students first discussed their design ideas and came to consensus. Then they plunged into selecting brightly colored fabrics, sequins, and other materials, and worked together to make their ideas come to life. During the workshops, there was no disruptive behavior, and withdrawn students became actively involved. Displaying their banners also helped raise the students' self-esteem, and other students and teachers gained new respect for the students in the Cluster Program once their skillful and imaginative creations were displayed in prominent places around the school building.

Luis, a belligerent loner who was new to the Cluster Program, was always getting into fights.[1] But when we started the banner-making project, he joined right in. He was confident, imaginative, and skilled as an artist, and knew just what he wanted to create. He cut out shapes and helped others figure out where their designs could fit.

This activity helped develop a rapport between Luis and the other students. They respected his artistic ability and discovered that they needed his help, which changed his status in the group. Teachers told us that he was accepted by the other students and that they now included him in their play. "He's a changed kid," his father later told us. "He doesn't feel like an outsider any more."

After the second year of the Tribal Rhythms Program, the principal at the Harvard-Kent school declared that a dramatic change had taken place in the school: "Today, our special-needs students and bilingual children are accepted into the mainstream of life within the school."

---

[1] All student names in this article are pseudonyms.

In 1990, when we completed our work at Harvard-Kent, the banners still hung in the school hallways. Teachers were using the techniques that we introduced to develop curriculum collectively and to solve problems that face the school community.

The arts not only can support the social side of school life; they can transform the learning of basic skills as well. In 1983, we began a three-year project at the John Marshall School, a K–5 elementary school in Dorchester, Massachusetts, an ethnically mixed neighborhood of Boston. Here, the Tribal Rhythms Program focused on academic as well as social skills.

When we met with the teachers, they said they were concerned that the students at all grade levels often lacked important social and verbal skills. For instance, many first- and second-grade youngsters had trouble combining words to form full, expressive statements, which in turn limited the development of other academic skills. The older children tended to talk all at once, not listening to each other or to their teacher. Students did not get along with each other; for example, a task such as lining up and walking single file to the bathroom would disintegrate and result in the children running. The techniques the teachers usually used to deal with such problems no longer worked.

The children's limited social and verbal skills, combined with overcrowded classrooms, made teaching a chore. The teachers wanted skill-building activities that would hold students' attention. In the upper grades, for example, the teachers wanted to focus on writing skills with new ideas for making writing fun.

We spent two weeks out of each month at the Marshall School, involving all of the 650 students. Each student participated in at least one activity every three weeks, and teachers worked with us after school during monthly in-service workshops. Each workshop presented creative arts activities that teachers could use to reinforce academic skills. For example, mask-making involved following directions step by step, instrument-building required measurement skills, book-making motivated the students to write autobiographies, and presenting a successful dramatic performance encouraged students to develop their speaking and listening skills.

During an in-service workshop on dramatic activities for the classroom, teachers role-played and acted out skits. They used cue cards to act out a variety of humorous characters, while we coached them in timing, conveying emotion, vocal projection, and body language. Then we brainstormed ideas for using these drama techniques to improve students' language skills. Teachers' ideas ranged from playing telephone games to enhance reading and listening skills, to creating stories using spelling words, to interpreting roles from cue cards and acting out skits based on them. We helped the teachers refine their ideas into arts activities, which they then implemented in their classrooms.

One of our goals was to offer the teachers opportunities for creative expression that would build their own self-confidence. If they discovered the artist in themselves, their personal connection to the arts would help them to integrate the arts into their classroom curriculum. Thus, by participating in the arts activities themselves, the teachers who saw art as an intimidating, complicated, and mysterious process realized how simple these activities were and how easy it would be to use them in teaching their students.

To address the teachers' concern that students giggled and talked when they should be listening, we jointly developed activities that would motivate students to listen. For example, teachers introduced a "freeze word" each day — that is, a word not commonly used, like "cabbage," "Beethoven," or "aardvark," that they would say two or three times a day, at which time students would stop all conversation and movement, holding their bodies in whatever position they stopped in. Students had to pay attention so as not to miss the "freeze word" and realize they were still moving while everyone else had "frozen" in place. We followed up by developing a participatory performance, "The Tribe That Forgot How To Listen," in which the students acted out all the things that go wrong when people don't listen.

During our performances and workshops with students, teachers are often able to see their students in new ways. One teacher was amazed that Tanika, who was introverted in class and never raised her hand, led a whole group in a "sash dance," a movement activity in which students followed the movements of whichever student wore a sash that we passed from child to child. In order to lead the dance, Tanika had to take the initiative to make up a dance step and lead the group with everyone watching. The teacher could not believe that she was the same quiet, introverted girl, and from that point on she saw Tanika's potential for taking an active part in classroom activities.

During the third year of the project, teachers gained the skills and confidence to develop arts-based classroom activities on their own. A core group of teachers collaborated with us on a booklet to share with other teachers the activities we had jointly created. The *Teacher Artist Connection* (1986) takes readers step by step through classroom-tested arts activities designed for improving academic and social skills in the first to the fifth grades.[2] Activities included making a tin-can shaker; interviewing community people; showing feelings through movement; and creating friendship scrapbooks, pen-pal projects, and a "drumming numbers" game.

[2] Cooperative Artists Institute, *Teacher Artist Connection* (Jamaica Plain, MA: Author, 1986).

As developers of the Tribal Rhythms Program, we believe that a new approach to educating today's children is needed, and that the success of our educational system will in large part be measured in terms of how well we teach our children to be critical thinkers and creative problem-solvers. We believe the arts can be a catalyst for this kind of change.

As the U.S. population becomes increasingly more ethnically diverse, we need to keep in mind what we have in common while also respecting our differences. To capitalize on this diversity and prepare our children for the future, our schools need leadership and innovative planning for change. Tribal Rhythms provides new approaches to help teachers and principals create community, reduce racial and social isolation, build self-esteem, and improve academic achievement.

Our approach and methods are transferable. The Tribal Rhythms thematic framework and community-building techniques can help educators at every grade level to create socially inclusive learning environments, to achieve their educational goals, and to prepare children for the challenges of the future.

Working from the Inside Out: A Practical Approach to Expression

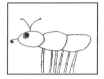

MARGOT GRALLERT

McCarthy-Towne is one of four elementary schools in Acton, Massachusetts. It was founded in 1971 by educators who believe that students' motivation to work and grow begins with their internal desire to do so. They believe it is more important for teachers to give direction to students as individuals than to use methods that guarantee uniformity or satisfy requirements for external goals or rewards. Pleasing oneself rather than others and working for one's own personal best rather than for someone else's judgment are important concepts for McCarthy-Towne parents, faculty, and students. McCarthy-Towne, unlike the other three elementary schools in Acton, was founded on this premise, which is the school's single most important educational concern.

The phrase "working from the inside out" gives form to this concept, which requires three conditions:

1. a belief that every person has an inner sense of self that can and must provide direction for learning;
2. an environment that encourages and stimulates the individual to find his or her personal direction;
3. a conviction that there are no final answers.

Working from the inside out is an individually directed thought process, an unpremeditated search for an unknown reality. It is a way of figuring out something that is your own.

Communication of an inside-out thought process is a personal expression. In order to learn to express their experience of an inside-out thought process, students need access to communication tools such as spoken or written language. Students then need time to practice using these tools repeatedly

Harvard Educational Review   Vol. 61   No. 3   August 1991

until they become skilled in their use. Students need guidance from people who have used the tools and who can present them in a way that allows for experimentation and discovery. This is the job of teachers, a job that has been a major focus of educators at McCarthy-Towne.

Acton is a predominately White, upper-middle-class community twenty-five miles west of Boston. Its educational system has an open enrollment policy that allows parents to choose which of the four elementary schools they want their children to attend. The four Acton schools receive equal funding, fulfill the same system requirements regarding testing and curriculum, and offer the same range of services for all Acton children. McCarthy-Towne differs from the other three schools in its faculty's choice of how to use funds and how to meet objectives that have received administrative support. They have chosen to work with each other and with consultants to design a curriculum that provides both direction and discovery, rather than to use texts and procedures that ensure specific results. In order to discourage the idea of finality and competition, the McCarthy-Towne faculty holds parent-teacher conferences instead of giving grades. At all times, the school atmosphere encourages activity rather than passivity and emphasizes process rather than product. The faculty believed in 1971, as they do today, that students need to be actively involved in and responsible for their own learning. Classrooms are designed for small-group activity at study centers, where children work independently. The children are given frequent choices and are expected to assume control over the management of their time, the completion of their work, and the smooth operation of the classroom.

Regular classroom meetings provide a forum for discussion of classroom activities. Children learn about what they need to work on at the study centers and which group, if any, will be working with the teacher. Working independently at a center with two or three others requires cooperation and trust. Being able to talk with others similarly involved about one's own work, seeing how others work, and giving and receiving help from peers encourages individual confidence and development. Individuality is the source of working from the inside out, and learning through doing is the process. In order for students to be involved in this process, they must have the time to practice using the tools so that they can learn to express what is on their minds.

All children in Acton go to the same junior high. From there through high school, McCarthy-Towne students readily adapt and conform to a more competitive educational environment. Teachers at these levels refer to McCarthy-Towne students as "imaginative" and "risk takers." They perform equally well as students from the other elementary schools on quantitative tests, and surveys of former McCarthy-Towne students indicate an appreciation for the quality of educational life they experienced at McCarthy-Towne.

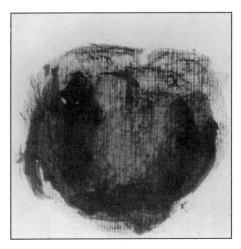 

Drawing from the inside out (left) and from the outside in

However, there is not yet any concrete way to measure the value of that experience.

The faculty applies the concept of working from the inside out not only to the way they work with students, but also to themselves. In 1971, they were convinced that experience and learning should not be compartmentalized. They wanted to develop their own insights about the artistic process rather than have a specialist teach Art as a separate subject. I was hired to help the faculty understand the value of doing artwork as it related to students and education.

I discovered that, just as no two students or teachers are alike, every classroom is unique both in its environment and in how curriculum is implemented. Thus, the work I did with teachers had to be as individually designed as the work each teacher did. Not knowing what to expect, I had to proceed by trial and error, and it was only later that I could reflect on why I made certain decisions and how I accommodated rather than compromised the value of doing artwork in school. Considering these reflections, I came to realize that:

1. No matter what I, myself, did in working with children and art, it was not as important to the children as what they did with their classroom teacher. Therefore, their teacher needed to be involved — not by supervising the artwork, but by showing concern, care, and support for the activity.

2. Artwork had to be done in the classroom in a manner consistent with any other schoolwork — as an independent responsibility that took time

and practice. Only then could students develop the skills to use the materials.

3. The art materials and instructions for their use had to be simple. They could neither interfere with the reason for using them (the focus of the artist's observation), nor complicate the constraints of the classroom, such as limited space or lack of water for paints.

These were the limits, the facts of the matter. The heart of the matter, the value of doing artwork, was more difficult to identify. It was less a question of what to do than of what *not* to do. Though I could not define what art was, I knew to begin with what I was convinced it was not. And art as education was not, I believe, one of two opposing views held by educators and artists, but rather two perspectives that needed to be understood.

Art with a capital "A" suggests that it is a product, something that is finished. In our answer-oriented culture, we overanalyze Art by trying to figure out what it's supposed to mean or how much it's worth. In this definition, the value is external and superficial; the same kind of value is represented by test scores and achievement awards in an educational context. Artists more often refer to their work with a small "a," indicating that art is a process that cannot be explained but that must be understood through experience. For artists, doing artwork is an exercise that may give them ideas for what to do next. The response the rest of us have to artwork is individual; it might be different for any person or culture at any given moment. Doing and understanding artwork, from the artist's and from the audience's perspectives, is an inside-out experience.

These two conflicting perspectives relate to art and education. Too much concern with how a product is made inhibits expression. Educators too often teach technique, directing the use of materials in lock-step procedures that guarantee a particular outcome, and assuming that if students practice enough of the rules, they will be able to "do art." Art in education often emphasizes what can be controlled; art as expression is often considered an uncontrollable, thoughtless, or "mindless" process.

Control is an instructional concern in all areas of traditional elementary school curricula, where making a finished, polished product is considered the most important outcome. Control is especially severe in Art class because there is so little time to practice the rules; something has to be made in a short period of time, perhaps as little as thirty minutes every other week. This forces the art teacher to show students what their work should look like — often by demonstration, sometimes by doing the work for them, and other times by giving students drawings to color in. There is no other way, because there is not enough time. Administrators, whose experience with art education is similar, want to see the results presented neatly and uniformly. The conformity important for spelling and multiplication tables is often also expected of art projects. Individuality is usually discouraged and, even when allowed, is often misunderstood.

The following example illustrates how individuality can be misunderstood. Children in a first-grade class made fun of a bird drawn by one of the students. The entire background was colored in with solid green grass-like strokes, and the bird was standing with its beak open in song. They made comments such as, "The grass shouldn't be in back of the bird, it should be under him," or, "It looks like he has grass in his mouth!" Everyone else's illustrations had an inch or two of green on the bottom with the bird standing on it; the rest of the paper was left white except for the sun in one corner. The teacher in this case did not help the others see this student's point of view. Thus the student, who actually had the keenest sense of a bird standing on the ground as well as the ability to express it, was left with a sense that somehow the illustration was wrong. There was no communication. The others could not see.

This was the kind of situation I hoped to avoid at McCarthy-Towne. I decided to call doing artwork "graphic exercise" rather than "Art" in order to eliminate any preconceptions about product or expression. I also did not use the vocabulary of Art, such as texture or form, or use what I considered empty words like "imaginative," "creative," or "beautiful" when discussing children's work. For me, such words had no meaning in education when I started working at McCarthy-Towne.

I set up graphic observation centers in classrooms where students could illustrate either something they were looking at or ideas they had that had no concrete form. Sometimes they were asked to create a picture of an object or a still life, and sometimes they were asked to show the abstract quality of a condition, such as weather or motion. The ideas used at these centers came at random from thoughts a teacher had, perhaps about a curriculum or an art material the teacher wanted to try. There was little that was as consistent or coherent as a lesson plan. With regard to the concept of working from the inside out, we, the educators, were not entirely sure of what we were doing.

As we watched ourselves, however, we found reasons to take the next step — to change, to adapt, or to cancel an idea. We teachers, who were guides for the students, had to create an environment that would allow individual expression. Our job was always to work without preconception of what the result should be. I was able to help the teachers because, fortunately, I did not have to explain what I was doing; I could show them. I was aware of what children were trying to do because I had experience with the same materials.

There was a particular concern, directly related to the definition of Art with a capital "A," that caused the classroom teachers at McCarthy-Towne to believe they couldn't teach or understand art. It was the final barrier that had to be eliminated to give the teachers and students access to artistic experience. This concern can be understood best in both a historical and an educational context.

The teachers at McCarthy-Towne who allowed ample time and space for art activities in the classrooms considered drawing to be the qualifying and absolute measure of all good artwork. To them, good drawing meant controlling a line with precision and detail so that the artwork created was accurate and representational. Perhaps because paper, pencils, and erasers were the tools common to all curriculum areas, drawing was considered the language of art; the best drawers were, thus, the best artists. Because of the historical context in which it was used to form numbers and letters, drawing meant creating lines. It encouraged control. I made a breakthrough in my own work with teachers when I found ways to alter their belief that linear drawing defined who was and was not an artist.

In retrospect, I recognize that I avoided the word "drawing," using color rather than line tools for most of the art exercises. From the earliest day to the present, I have asked students to start their artwork "in the middle." They understand that to mean, literally, the center of what they are looking at, such as the nose or surface of the face of an animal in a photograph or the red of the apple in a still life. They know to let their work grow from that place, although they may choose the particular place to start. For an abstract representation such as cold and frozen or hot and swirling, they may use chalks and watercolors. They experiment over and over again until they find their own expression of the condition. In either case, they begin with only a literal point of visual reference or an undefined concept. The idea that there has to be a particular method or a preconceived plan of action in art was an obstacle to understanding artwork.

Set answers and uniformity might be appropriate to spelling and multiplication tables, where consistency can provide a basis for being able to use words and numbers. Working from the inside out, however, is vitally different: it has only a beginning. Working this way permits personal expression. The art of artwork lies in personal expression and experience. The value of art, I believe, is only in the process of making and/or experiencing it.

In practice, however, there must be a balance between the two definitions of Art and art: between craftsmanship — the skill to use the tools — and expression — the ability to "say" something. The McCarthy-Towne classroom structure gives students the time necessary to do both. Discussion about the nature of the object that is being observed requires students to focus on expression. Art materials that make it difficult to outline, confine, or correct give students access to the artistic process. Given time to use the tools, they learn the skills they need in order to express themselves.

Learning how to observe carefully teaches understanding. Without that awareness there is little communication between teachers and students, either with artwork or written work. If observation had been important in the previous example of the first-grade bird illustrations, those students would have understood and learned from the one piece of work they made fun of. But this takes time, and children tend to rush through their work if the teacher does not understand. A McCarthy-Towne teacher noticed a dramatic increase in the time one child was spending at the art center; when she asked why, the child replied: "Because I learned how to see."

With this understanding, we now use traditional vocabulary to discuss art at McCarthy-Towne. We recognize art as a process. We see drawing in color rather than just line. We understand such terms as texture and form because we see how they contribute to expression. Both spoken and written language have come to be used to understand the value of artwork at McCarthy-Towne.

Specific comments can indicate how working from the inside out has helped teachers and their students:

> It's different discovering techniques for yourself because you experiment as opposed to learning that there are tricks. There's a danger of getting hooked on doing just the tricks.

> Students learn from each other. They see how others are trying things, coming up with ideas, making breakthroughs.

> They are appreciative of each other's artwork. It's not which one is best, but which ones are successful in different ways.

> It encourages what you have in yourself. You just need to get it out. . . . If it's not recognized, there's no realization of what talents he or she has.

> I learn so much about the kids by the choices they make — how they go about it.

> It's only mine and only I could have done that. That's what I like to see in a kid's work.

> I enjoy the beauty of different responses.

These are the kinds of observations that guide and support us. In order to understand how we do specific art exercises, it is important to know how I work with teachers. The collaboration is constantly changing, and is always unique to a particular classroom. Some teachers work entirely on their own. In such cases, I simply help them decide on the materials they will need. In other classrooms, either the teacher or I may lead a discussion of what is happening at an art center. Sometimes I help teachers integrate art activities with other activities, such as in social studies or science, and sometimes I suggest activities just "for art's sake."

I am in the school for three hours every morning. Unless I need to be at a class meeting, my time is unscheduled; most of it is spent moving from room to room, checking on what's happening, and making changes if needed. Though I am ultimately responsible for setting up and implementing the centers in the classrooms that need my help, I always consider the input of teachers and students. As one teacher comments: "Kids are often the ones to make the extensions. They are not intimidated by limited choices and will ask for a different material if they think it would work better. Things take turns we often don't anticipate, and often for the better."

Working from the inside out can now be explained in light of its application at McCarthy-Towne for skill development and craftsmanship. Specific art exercises demonstrate how we accommodate rather than compromise the value of doing artwork. There are three important elements to this application:

1. the focus of the observation;

2. the art materials that are best suited to the observation;

3. the cognitive and expressive value of the artwork.

In order to clarify how color is used, an example that uses the simplest materials may be helpful. Most schoolwork is done with graphite pencil and white paper. Though the negative space of the white paper is irrelevant to a written story or numbers and answers, positive and negative space are equally important to visual artwork. When students work on colored paper or work with colored materials, they consider the space they are working on as important as what they impose on that space.

They most often analyze the color, form, shape, and texture of scientific specimens or cultural artifacts with colored media. The colors are specific to what is being observed, and the students are asked to let the color of the paper show through where it contributes to the color or texture of the object.

Working this way with artwork helps students see that the process and the result work together. Unlike written work, what they add is affected by what is already there. There is always a balance between the two. Art, written or visual, is a whole experience, not fragments of information. Composition has meaning for both art forms. A good written composition is complete because of the words alone. Composition in graphic art, however, means that the whole visual piece must work together because it has physical form.

The instructions and the materials for classroom centers are carefully structured to focus students' observation. In the study of shells at the first-grade level, for instance, the focus is quite specific. There might be two or three media involved, and students might draw only the different kinds of lines there are in a clam, a scallop, and a mussel. But to capture the myriad and iridescent colors of the interior of an abalone shell, students might combine colored sticks and watercolor. They start their artwork in the middle and discover how to show not only the colors, but also the hard swirling texture.

When observing an artifact, students may do several exercises with different media. Second graders are given the four colors they need to analyze the patterns in Kente cloth from Ghana. The paper they work on is cut to the size they need to show one segment of the cloth, and the whole of the paper is colored. Then they actually weave their own interpretation of the pattern, doing as many as two or three weavings that measure four by ten inches. They are given the time to experiment, to see if they can show diagonals, or to decide how many strings they need to use to make a consistent pattern.

The value in these exercises is less in the expression than it is in the development of concrete observational skills. With these skills, students gain the accuracy and confidence to express their own individual perception.

Art exercises start very simply. In a study of Japan, first graders use watercolor to discover ways that brush, black paint, and water can work together. They may spend two or three days just trying to produce dark and light, and another two or three on producing different kinds of strokes. They use the medium extensively until it becomes second nature to them.

Later on, when they study the desert, they use a combination of watercolor, chalk, and collage to illustrate their own idea of what a nighttime or daytime desert environment might be like. They become familiar with all three media because of frequent use, and can discuss how they might use the soft, dry, or liquid qualities of chalk and watercolor. They decide where collage (gluing down paper pieces) can be used best — perhaps to express mountains, animals, or the sky.

When these same students read Hopi mythology in second grade, they use the same materials to express concepts concerning ancient stories of the Indians' struggle to exist in time and space. They illustrate sentences from different myths, such as: "The world began to spin around crazily, then rolled over twice. Mountains plunged into seas with a great splash. Seas and lakes sloshed over the land. As the world spun through cold and lifeless space, it froze into solid ice." Or, "Then all was quiet, and they knew they were floating."

Tempera paint is often used as a means of self-expression. Students start with simple beginnings. In kindergarten, they paint only with shades of red for one week, then only with blue for another. When they mix paint to make the color of a fall leaf, it is only the leaf's color they are working on, not its shape. In third grade, they may paint the sky seen from their classroom window — every day, morning and afternoon, for months. This enables them to discover color and atmosphere, literally and expressively. From their own work, and through a study of impressionism, they then learn to see the moods paint can create; they learn to understand expression.

Students are able to work expressively when they do not have to stop and think. When students are too concerned with a step-by-step approach to doing artwork, it becomes too much of a conscious effort. This is why the focus, both of what is being asked and of the materials offered, is extremely important. There are, of course, limits inherent in these exercises. But these limits are inherent in the tools the students are working with and in what they experience through observation, not in their preconceptions.

By communicating a personal experience through artwork to their teachers and classmates, students discover that their hands know a lot that their heads didn't know they knew. If there is too much planned control, personal vision can be destroyed. Conversely, too little control can give the medium too much power. Because students are given enough time to practice with the materials, they gain craftsmanship; because the craftsmanship does not interfere, they and their teachers realize the importance of expression.

At McCarthy-Towne, as in most schools, we ask children to tell us about the three-dimensional world they are experiencing. We ask them to translate their experience into two-dimensional media by incorporating art with verbal language and other sequential information without compromise. By working from the inside out with two-dimensional (especially color) materials, students are able to think comprehensively. Perhaps they can remain actively engaged in a three-dimensional world when art materials for expression are offered in such a way as to catch them off guard, as it were, in order to forestall any possible preconceptions.

To keep the artwork experiential and at the same time develop cognitive and expressive skills, students need time and practice. Students should have to work through the materials in order to see what happens, as in the following example: When first graders illustrate how an island is formed, they work on strips of colored paper approximately six by twenty inches. The strips are folded in equal segments of four or five inches, and a line is drawn two inches from the bottom along the length of each strip. In each segment, the students illustrate conditions that need to happen in order for an island to grow. The illustrations are done above the line, and the words go below. The first illustration may show swirls of blue, dark and light, with a solid area or line. The words might read, "a rumbling crack broke open in the bottom of the ocean." Another segment might include a volcano and, finally, an island. Using colored sticks and watercolor in combination, students fill in the illustrated segments completely, letting the paper color show through only where it is relevant to the story. The written work is done after the artwork, because students use more descriptive language when writing about their artwork than when they write first and illustrate afterwards.

Working from the inside out as a community and individually is a circular rather than a linear concept. The climate of McCarthy-Towne supported who

I was so I could proceed without knowing what I was going to do. I could in turn provide discovery and direction that supported a way of working in which we all believed. I was able to work this way before I tried to explain it. I discovered the phrase "working from the inside out" by asking children to do artwork that way, then I realized it applied to the way we faculty work as well. With confidence and trust, we start with our own inner sense of self to observe and encourage the students we work with to do the same thing.

In its broadest and most critical sense, working from the inside out has more to do with the philosophical foundation of the school than it does with the materials and procedures in the art program. As one teacher put it, at McCarthy-Towne "a form of individual expression has been allowed to flourish." It thrives because it is an ever-changing phenomenon. As long as students have the time to explore from a personal vantage point, expression can be developed by using the tools, the media, and the systems available to them. Working from the inside out is at once comprehensive and compatible with the cultural and educational resources familiar to students and teachers. Working from the inside out is an open-ended conclusion, a concept that relies not on methodology or procedures, but on inspiration.

Computer-Aided Collaborative Music Instruction

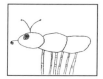

JAMES A. HOFFMANN

For about twenty years, I have taught a traditional music harmony course at the New England Conservatory. As an experiment, I adapted this course for collaborative learning using Macintosh computers. It was apparent from the beginning of my experiment that these computers could greatly facilitate the teaching of harmony. As the course unfolded, it became clear that using the computer for managing music need not be restricted to music students and professionals: computers render the composition and performance of music accessible to greatly increased numbers of people, even those without extensive musical training. The growing availability of computers thus carries a profound significance for altering the role of music in society. Their versatility provides the means for changing a common attitude that has become entrenched in this century — that the activities of musicians lack relevance to society. The microcosm of the conservatory harmony class demonstrates one way in which the activities of musicians can be reintegrated into society.

In this article, I begin by considering the potential of computer-aided music learning to integrate the roles of composer, performer, and listener, which are presently separated in Western classical music. Next I review traditional harmony instruction, its position in the music curriculum and common method of instruction. I have implemented one solution to the dilemma of this separation of musical roles by adapting a standard harmony course to a computer-aided collaborative learning format, which I describe in detail. After a discussion of the activities in the Computer Studio where this experiment took place and an evaluation of the material used, I close the article with a discussion of the evaluation of this new approach and a summary of student reactions.

Harvard Educational Review   Vol. 61   No. 3   August 1991

Computer-Aided Music in Society

Music, a potent social instrument from earliest times, operates not merely in imitation of society but also in dynamic interaction with it. In comprehending this, a performing musician gains power not only over his or her immediate audience, but, through contemporary media, over a much broader public as well — for good or ill. Although the pop star Madonna behaves as *she* pleases, through her performances she impels young women to emulate her. One of her fans writes:

> I'm a 16-year-old who thinks of Madonna as a role model. While many parents don't share my opinion, they should know that she got good grades in high school and managed to make it in New York City. If that's not the kind of determination parents are looking for in their kids, then I don't know what is. So what if she's outrageous?[1]

This is indeed a potent image for our youth. Another example is the message the rap group Public Enemy sends Black youth, one "of Black pride and Afro-centrism [that] informs their politics and attitudes and . . . serves as a source of information on Black history and current events."[2] For example, the refrain to their song *Fear of the Black Planet* addresses White man's fear of a relationship between his daughter, or sistah [*sic*], or wife and a Black man. It gives dignity and integrity to Black man and suggests reasons why White man ought to change his attitude:

> Excuse us for the news
> You might not be amused
> But did you know White comes from Black
> No need to be confused

> Excuse us for the news
> I question those accused
> Why this fear of Black from White
> Influence who you choose?

The music works in two complementary ways: through its appeal it attracts a community of listeners who are open to its message, which in turn gathers its full impact from the music. The music articulates and impressively conveys the feelings expressed by the words. Thus the performance as a whole force-

---

[1] Omer Kamran, Letter to the Editor, *USA WEEKEND*, September 14–16, 1990, p. 12, in response to an interview with Madonna ("Totally Outrageous," June 8–10, 1990). See also Camille Paglia, "Madonna: Finally, a Real Feminist," Op-Ed, *New York Times*, December 14, 1990, and Caryn James, "Beneath All That Black Lace Beats the Heart of a Bimbo . . . ," *New York Times*, December 16, 1990, p. 38.

[2] Kevin Cullen, "When Public Enemy Raps, Many Hub Youths Get the Message," *Boston Globe*, May 30, 1990, p. 1. See also Jon Pareles, "'Radical' Rap: Of Pride and Prejudice," *New York Times*, December 16, 1990, p. 1.

fully addresses both the intellect and the emotions simultaneously. While pop culture is seldom addressed in conservatory training, these examples illustrate vividly the social power of musical performance. A major function of art in the broadest sense is the continual offering of our collective self-understanding for public acceptance. The arts that use time as a primary medium — music, dance, drama — consist of three actions: creation, performance, and reception. Creation, the heart of artistic activity, can only persist in the presence of validation, which is the primary role of the listener or receiver. Between these two roles stands the mediating function of performance and performer. In Western classical music during the nineteenth century, the actions of composing, performing, and listening became increasingly separate. Performers became separate from creators, and the public, or audience, took on the primary listener/evaluator role. In Western classical music, that segment of the public consisting of critics, agents, competition judges, grant-givers, and the like plays a significant and sometimes decisive part in the evaluation/validation process.

This fundamentally artificial stratification has led to the popular misconception that composers and performers function outside the social mainstream. General society, in turn, feels cut off from participation in the composer and performer roles. Through a process of marginalization, this results in a degradation of the entire music enterprise, which is then assumed to be peripheral to what many apparently consider "important activities" of modern life. When public monies become severely limited, funds for artistic endeavors are among the first items cut from budgets. This may be observed, for example, in the public schools, where music is often considered a "frill" that can easily be removed without serious detriment to students.[3] Modern society is generally business-oriented, supported by and supportive of the sciences and technology. Most performers and composers of classical music are not part of this picture, yet many of them feel compelled to make music despite the lack of compensation. This is neither understood nor accepted by a society motivated largely by material concerns.

Devaluation of the musical function shows a widespread lack of awareness of the depths of social and psycho-intellectual processes that are opened to exploration and clarification through creating and performing music. The major functions of the performing arts have been, for much of the world, "the process . . . of making the hidden visible, the latent manifest, the inaudible audible, the stilled dynamic," and "of making the intransigent tractable."[4]

---

[3] See Alan Lupo, "The Culture Cutters," Op-Ed, *Boston Globe*, May 11, 1991.

[4] Robert Plant Armstrong, *The Powers of Presence: Consciousness, Myth, and Affecting Presence* (Philadelphia: University of Pennsylvania Press, 1980), p. 20.

Computers provide an easily accessible means to compose and perform music, enabling all who so desire to create and perform, individually or collectively. The public, which carries the evaluating role, can thus gain a greater understanding of musical processes and deepen its ability to evaluate composition and performance. This accessibility provided by computers has the power to restore music-making to its vital function in society, once again opening its profound resources to everyone.

The practice of music has the potential not only to suggest directions for balancing some of the divisive forces at work in society today, but also the capacity to generate restorative action through participation. An individual achieves social status through the act of performance and intellectual development through the act of preparing for performance. On the social level, it is not possible to perform as a group without some measure of mutual respect among its members, nor is it fulfilling to perform before an unreceptive audience. Thus, a mutual bond is forged among members of a performing group and between performers and audiences.

Conservatory training has contributed to the isolation of musical processes. A conservatory's principal activity is to train performers. This involves working one-on-one with a performer/teacher to acquire performance skills and traditions — a slow and arduous process. In contrast, the smaller group of composition students at the conservatory perform rarely, if at all, and are thus separated from the conservatory mainstream. In the conservatory, then, we have a microcosm of the relation of musicians to society where the primary evaluation/validation role is filled by the studio teacher or faculty jury.

Various music theory courses, among which harmony is of primary importance, have traditionally provided an avenue for addressing the separation of the composer/performer/listener functions that is less than adequate. As taught at most conservatories, harmony is based on the music of a small group of composers who lived in a limited area of Europe during a short historical period. The music of these composers — from Bach to Brahms — forms the standard repertoire of Western classical musicians. This narrow focus relegates much of today's music, in all its stylistic variety and cultural scope, to the periphery of the typical conservatory curriculum. Harmony courses, then, consist of learning to compose musical phrases derived primarily from the common practices of the aforementioned composers. Students understand this as learning to use sets of arbitrary procedures and their variants. In reality, these procedures constitute the conventions of tonal music. Many students rarely hear their work, and often do not understand what they write. For them, an evaluation determines merely whether the "rules" have been followed or whether the instructor subjectively judges their work to be "correct." This practice, however, is remote from actual composition and has, unfortunately, promoted rather than ameliorated the separation of musical functions.

A music computer studio offers a way for performers, composers, and interested members of the public to integrate musical activities. At the conservatory level, performers who work in collaborative groups can develop an understanding of the craft of music composition and thereby acquire access to the creative function. The computer can instantly replay — that is, "perform" — composed music, enabling the group to criticize and revise their work before submitting it to the instructor for evaluation. For the individual student composer, the computer's playback capability provides an easy means for hearing his or her work. Outside the conservatory, the access to musical activities provided by computers can help any interested person or group of people to become an independent musical force limited only by human imagination and the culture's acceptance of the results.

Traditional Harmony

The New England Conservatory's multinational student body comes with varied pre-collegiate training in music skills other than performing or composing in classical or jazz styles. Students enroll in first-year preparatory music theory studies prior to taking a one-year, sophomore-level harmony course. The harmony course is designed to give students a feel for tonal materials, to train their eyes to recognize written tonal patterns, and to sensitize their ears to standard tonal relations. These skills are vital to a musician, since they provide criteria for interpreting tonal music.

Harmony is typically taught through assignments using the chorale (hymn) texture of four voices — soprano, alto, tenor, and bass. Students learn about types and uses of chords (groups of tones sounded together), and, by shaping the melodic lines of the four voices, how to form progressions of chords. They are asked to harmonize melodies (sopranos) or basses (lowest voices) of musical phrases and submit assignments to the instructor for correction and grading. In my harmony course I incorporate an approach called "functional harmony," which classifies chords according to the purpose each fulfills in the tonal structure.[5] Class time is used to present new material with models, evaluate student work, and analyze appropriate passages from the music of relevant composers.

---

[5] Two recent articles on functional harmony are Marion A. Guck, "The Functional Relations of Chords: A Theory of Musical Intuitions," *in theory only*, 4, No. 6 (1978), 29–42; and Charles J. Smith, "Prolongations and Progressions as Musical Syntax," in *Musical Theory — Special Topics*, ed. Richmond Browne (New York: Academic Press, 1981), pp. 156–167.

Adaptation for Computer-Aided Learning

The objective of my computer-aided harmony course is to enable students to create their own harmonic phrases, including sopranos and basses.[6] For practical purposes, work in the Computer Studio (approximately half of the classes) is confined to the construction of short harmonic patterns, since there is insufficient studio time for a group of students to compose even one complete six- to eight-measure phrase with refined results in all the details of chord choice, harmonic rhythm, and the quality of soprano and bass melodic lines. These patterns are vehicles for learning to use a series of sequentially introduced chords. In the classroom, conventional uses of the featured chords of each unit are explained and illustrated by the instructor. During the Studio class period, students do sets of exercises incorporating these chords.

At the conclusion of each unit, students independently compose complete musical phrases in which harmonic patterns are embedded and submit their phrases as homework to the instructor for evaluation. Here, the use of the computer is optional, a choice only recently available to students. However, use of the computer's playback capacity enables students to hear the assignment in progress, instead of merely following "rules" while having at best a vague impression of the resulting sound. Classroom quizzes and final examinations require the composition of complete harmonic phrases.

Working in the Computer Studio

New England Conservatory harmonic classes have up to twenty students. A maximum of three students work at each computer in the Computer Studio. The student groups vary in makeup and are changed periodically. After each Computer Studio class, the students copy the day's exercises onto a personal disk. When groups are disbanded, one member copies their exercises onto a "community disk," which the instructor then reviews to assess the progress of that group.

The activity of classes in the Computer Studio follows a general pattern. First, one group member reads the assignment aloud from the syllabus. The students then discuss the assignment among themselves, after which the student at the computer control notates the first chord of the first exercise onto the computer screen — a standard opening chord, the tonic. Next, the stu-

---

[6] The composer Arnold Schoenberg (1874–1951) advocated this creative approach to teaching harmony in his *Theory of Harmony,* translated by Roy E. Carter (Berkeley: University of California Press, 1978), pp. 13–17. This book was originally published in 1911.

dents identify the featured chord of the exercise together with its method of introduction, then enter the chord as specified. Finally, the chord or chords that should follow the featured chord are determined by the students and entered. After an exercise is completed, it is "performed" by the computer, and the students evaluate its sound. During this process, the instructor is always available to clarify the assignment and to answer questions that may arise. When one or more exercises have been finished, the instructor listens to the music and asks for students' comments. Sounds that students do not like are often the result of failure to follow the conventions of tonal music. The instructor either approves the work or requests correction.

Students take turns at the computer controls with each exercise. When the set of exercises has been finished and has received final approval, students save the assignments on individual disks.

Software

The harmony course uses the Deluxe Music Construction Set (DMCS) software, a straightforward music notation program for creating simple scores. This program is advantageous for the harmony course, because even students with no computer experience can readily use it without special training classes. Harmony exercises start at once, and students quickly acquire the ability to use the program to enter and remove notes in the context of their work. A special feature of DMCS is that the pitches can sound as they are entered or moved about on the computer screen. This creates an instant correlation between a pitch symbol and its referent sound, which enables students to compose by ear and immediately connect what they hear to the written version produced by the computer. The studio setup allows for the amplification of computer-originated sounds by external speakers. Computers that are attached to synthesizers allow students to hear the effect of exercises played with a variety of instrumental sounds.

Evaluation of Computer-Aided Learning

A significant advantage of the computer-aided approach to teaching is that students work on assignments together *during* class time; in traditional harmony courses, these assignments would have been done outside of class as individual homework. This is a clear time advantage for music students, whose professional goals require them to spend long periods practicing, rehearsing, and performing. Furthermore, work in class is produced under the guidance of an instructor, whose immediate help is far superior to the time-delayed written comments students would otherwise receive, which may not be understood and thus cannot contribute to the improvement of student skills.

In a regular classroom situation, individual help is often precluded by time and space limitations. Collaborative work that might be done at the blackboard is limited by lack of space, and, furthermore, ten to fifteen minutes of class time would be needed simply to copy work from the board. In contrast, the Computer Studio easily accommodates seven groups of two or three students working together without the constraints of a traditional classroom setting.

The greatest advantage of teaching harmony with the use of computers is its aural feedback feature. (As noted earlier, this is a key element in the reintegration of music into society.) In the traditional class without this feature, students often submit harmony homework with little knowledge of how it sounds. This significantly hinders progress, and is a point at which traditional instruction breaks down. Many undergraduates have not yet developed the ability to read harmonic progressions silently, and those who lack adequate keyboard skills cannot play them on the piano. Understanding how harmonic patterns function, which is the goal of harmony instruction, depends on the development of aural sensitivity to these patterns. This process is greatly facilitated by the playback capacity of the computer, which means that students no longer need to present unheard, unrevised work to an instructor.

In collaborative learning, students virtually teach one another. They reinforce the teacher's instructions, and share in decisionmaking and in evaluating results. The learning of harmony becomes a shared, ongoing, and externalized process, comparable to a performance. By this means, students achieve an educational objective through step-by-step assimilation of chord vocabulary and uses. In striking contrast to the traditional classroom, which is often characterized by a passive attitude among students, students in the Computer Studio enter into lively discussions while solving the problems presented by the exercises. Each group must arrive at a consensus on what is entered into the computer and on their assessment of the finished work after hearing it "performed" by the computer.

From an instructor's point of view, the collaborative method is quite different from the conventional classroom in which the teacher is "on stage," a performer controlling the activity and pace of the course, while the students assume the audience role. In the Computer Studio, teacher and students work in a cooperative environment. The instructor is, in effect, an ex-officio member of each group, dividing time among them and being available to all. The instructor acts as a guide — providing directions, mediating disputes, and evaluating students' work. His or her role in the proceedings is less remote and less dominant than that of the traditional lecturer; the student-teacher interaction of the collaborative situation is also more demanding on the instructor than the structured, controlled classroom practices. His or her reward is the students' sense of achievement, which is clearly evident in their reactions to their work.

The results of a blind questionnaire given after the first semester of the second year of this experiment were overwhelmingly positive. Fourteen of eighteen students returned the questionnaire, and twelve answered all eleven questions. One hundred percent of the respondents said they would choose to continue doing assignments in the Computer Studio rather than return to the traditional method of instruction. Seventy-five to 100 percent of the students responded in the affirmative when asked whether working with computers and in groups was enjoyable, whether learning could be transferred from the classroom to the Computer Studio and vice versa, and whether immediately hearing results of their work was helpful in learning to associate symbol and sound. The following student comments, some of which have been edited, illustrate students' responses to this approach to harmony. I have categorized their responses with reference to either collaborative learning or working with computers. The number in parentheses after each comment indicates the number of other students who made similar remarks.

Advantages of Collaborative Learning

> You learn more because you are exposed to other ideas and you need to compromise. . . . The group helps each other understand the assignment. (6)

> The teacher is right there to answer your questions and follow your progress so you don't get too confused or off track. (6)

> Active involvement of all students as opposed to passive reaction to what the teacher writes on the board [is helpful]. (1)

Disadvantages of Collaborative Learning

> I would rather have the groups comprised of two, as opposed to three, people — it's easier to communicate. (2)

> The ideal would be to work alone and at your own computer. (1)

> A little more time in class; I really don't feel I was actually taught in a classroom environment. (1)

> [I didn't like] having to teach the others in your group if they haven't done their reading, etc. (1)

Advantages of Working with a Computer

> One gets to hear the assignment right away and correct it when something sounds wrong. . . . Hearing the exercise immediately definitely helps me get a better idea of how the notes correspond to the sounds. (8)

One is able to correct exercises easily. . . . A person can try out different options for voice leading without messy erasures. (3)

Assignments come out neatly. (2)

You gain computer literacy. (1)

Disadvantages of Working with a Computer

I'm trying to force myself to hear in my head by myself. . . . These exercises should be played on the piano. (0)

It takes more time than writing it would by hand. . . . The controls can be tedious. (0)

Possible computer malfunction. (1)

Maybe time is wasted with disks and technical problems. (0)

The sounds are of low quality. (1)

Computers are confusing. (0)

Conclusion

In using computers as a tool for learning harmony, students progress through the vocabulary of traditional harmony by notating practice exercises in the New England Conservatory's Computer Studio and by applying these procedures in harmonic phrases they compose on their own. The Computer Studio makes possible guided collaborative learning and immediate aural feedback. Discussion within groups, the instructor's assistance, and the capacity for immediate evaluation of results all serve to help each student develop skills for managing harmony more effectively than do customary teaching methods. Students' actions in the Computer Studio, as well as their responses to the questionnaire, indicate a strong positive reaction to this approach.

Throughout most of human history, music has served to integrate societies. The separation of music's creator and performer functions is peculiar to contemporary Western culture. Leading first to stratification within the discipline, and ultimately to the marginalization and degradation of musicians by the social mainstream, this process has robbed the community of one of its basic means of expression and integration.

> Of all the artistic activities of the human race there is none which more closely puts us in touch with the sources of myth, or magic, of ritual and religion, none which more subtly outlines the forms of that potential society which lies still beyond our grasp [than music].[7]

---

[7] Christopher Small, *Music, Society, Education*, 2nd rev. ed. (London: John Calder, 1980), p. 227.

Modern computer technology now offers the means to restore the long historical tradition of musical practice to modern society. The collaborative learning experiment described in this article illustrates and exemplifies one way in which reintegration might be achieved.

Acknowledgement is due Lyle Davidson, Chairman of Undergraduate Theory at the New England Conservatory and Research Associate at Harvard Project Zero, for suggesting and encouraging my use of computers in the teaching of harmony; and to Paul Burdick, Director of the Conservatory's Music and Computer Studio (MACS), for his expert and generous assistance in developing this course. I would like to express my appreciation to them for making helpful suggestions regarding a draft of this article. I am indebted to Mary Ann Hoffmann, whose help in formulating this article was indispensable.

And Practice Drives Me Mad; or, the Drudgery of Drill

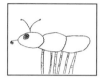

V. A. HOWARD

"TIPS for Success"

When it comes to the honing of skills and the stamping in of various habits and procedures, nothing beats sound instruction combined with assiduous drill. Practice makes perfect, the saying goes, especially for the highly gifted. Enshrined therein are two of the most commonplace clichés about learning used in the English language: that of native talent and its shaping by persistent repetition. Add to talent and practice the watchful eye of an instructor, and the formula is complete for success in the classroom, in the artist's studio, or on the playing field: Talent + Instruction + Practice = Success (TIPS).

Like most commonsense generalizations about learning, the TIPS formula is expressed in terms invitingly vague and ambiguous. Variations on TIPS are ubiquitous in educational thought, allotting different meaning and weight to each of the three casual terms: talent, instruction, and practice. For example, some proponents of early aptitude (Seashore, 1947), of IQ or genetically based intelligence (Jensen, 1972, 1981), and personality factors (Kagan & Brim, 1980) tend to stress the "givens" of human nature in learning. On the other hand, while disagreeing on most matters, behavioral and cognitive psychologists agree in stressing the "environmental" factors of instruction and practice (Skinner, 1965; Bruner, 1986). Interestingly, many art teachers and athletic coaches take the rather self-effacing view that talent (including personality factors like "ambition" and "toughness") plus practice, helped along by instructional nudges, primarily determine who will or will not succeed.

Harvard Educational Review   Vol. 61   No. 1   February 1991

More puzzling than any of the quarrels among psychologists and practitioners over teaching and learning complex skills is the reductive approach typical of much curriculum research and development. Aiming at quick results on the basis of an "empirical" interpretation of the TIPS formula, curriculum developers often view their task as threefold: first, using one set of criteria, they reduce all questions of gifts or talent to ones of measurable, fixed aptitudes or potential; second, by another set of criteria, they reduce all questions of instruction and training to technological ones of sufficient means to specifiable ends; and third, by reading off the formula for success from the behavior of those who have succeeded, they thereby convert *established* practice into *recommended* practice.[1]

While seeming to temper the wind to the shorn lamb, such tactics end by slaughtering the lamb. Issues of value and choice, of symbolism and interpretation, of judgment and understanding, of inquiry and discovery cannot easily be rendered down. Aside from the obvious confusion of the "is" with the "ought" of prevailing practice, an approach to learning skills (or to anything else for that matter) that assumes a) that potentials and aptitudes are more given than made, b) that they are changeless and nonconflicting in their development, and c) that they are value free in their higher cultivation and uses, is less scientific than scientistic.[2]

That this kind of social science fiction engenders mere "bags of tricks" is hardly noteworthy. What is noteworthy about all the aforementioned variations on the TIPS formula is their inattention to the several roles of imagination in learning; to the conceptual landscape of instruction; to the personal growth of performance standards; to the interpretive effort required to learn from one's mistakes; and, most conspicuously, to the nature of practice itself: learning to practice and practising to learn.[3]

The humblest term in the TIPS formula, practice is in fact a complex concept encompassing a range of sophisticated activities from finger drills to dress rehearsal, from rote memorization to critical strategy. Failure to

---

[1] Many doctoral theses and research proposals in education fall into this general pattern, not only in curriculum studies, but also in leadership, management, and policy studies. The tendency to a reductive, pseudo-empiricism is further exacerbated by the "request for proposal" documents emanating from private and government funding agencies. Whether researchers are pandering to agency preconceptions or the reverse is a chicken-and-egg question I happily bequeath to sociologists of knowledge.

[2] On the varieties and "myths" of potential in educational thought, see Israel Scheffler's *Of Human Potential* (1985). See also chapter five, "Knowledge and Skill," in his *Conditions of Knowledge* (1965/ 1985) and chapter six, "Practice and the Vision of Mastery," in my *Artistry: The Work of Artists* (1982). The latter two especially undergird much of the present discussion.

[3] These and other topics, including the complex relations among learning by instruction, by practice, by example, and by reflection, are explored in *Learning by All Means: Lessons from the Arts* (1992). For details on imagery and imaginal controls in learning, the reader is referred to my *Artistry* (1982, pp. 134–148). All I can offer here are a few basic distinctions about practice in general and what amounts to a plea for the dignity of drill.

grasp the subtleties of practice leads to oversimplification, as exemplified by the phrase "mere drill" on the one hand and, on the other, to overreliance on vague notions like gift, talent, knack, or inspiration to explain how advanced skills are mastered. I turn now to some enlightening ambiguities in the notion of practice.

Practice versus Practising

Hereinafter, I shall distinguish the noun, as in *a* or *the* practice, from the verb, as in *to* practise or practising. A (the) practice refers to an established or customary way of doing things. That may be a matter of accumulated knowledge and rational precedent, as in medicine or law; a matter of arbitrary convention, as with driving on the left or right; a matter of ritual and doctrine, as in religious practices; a matter of principle, as in moral practices; or a matter of culture, as with certain social practices (such as bowing or shaking hands). In these and similar instances, the practice represents the "done thing," what tradition, ritual, past experience, precedent, or lore dictates to us.

We should indeed be deprived without the established practices of the professions, disciplines, arts, and occupations. Some practices take the form of vast natural experiments and comprise the accumulated wisdom of a given field that gets passed on to succeeding generations of practitioners. In other forms, as conventions of etiquette, rules of parliamentary debate, or traffic regulations, established practices make up the "social grease" that facilitates the conduct of everyday life.

Little wonder, then, that practising is often construed as a way of handing on the establishment — of internalizing the done thing by drill, itself construed as a kind of obedient, mindless repetition. Examples from reciting multiplication tables to early moral and social conduct to military training readily come to mind as reflexive "second nature" behavior that has been stamped in by drill. Such acquired, automatic behavior of second nature is seen in turn to capitalize on the innate reactions of "first nature." Embedded in the aforementioned TIPS formula, such a view of practices and practising reinforces the notion of instruction and training as rote processes that demand compliance over critical interpretation. By this route, professional training in virtually any field comes to be seen as an inflexible, blinkered way of passing on entrenched knowledge and procedures. I shall argue against this view that practising is not limited to passing on *the* practice by drill, and that, even where that is the emphasis, drill is anything but mindless repetition.

I once visited a dental laboratory where student dentists were practising bridge-making techniques: bending the tiny wires just so, molding the prosthetic materials, and, incidentally, strengthening their fingers. They did this under the watchful eye of a senior technician, himself under the supervision of a dental surgeon. "You cannot afford to make a mistake like this once you are in practice," the technician crooned quietly as he examined a piece of student work. Again and again he gently admonished his students for this or that technical flaw, making corrections as he passed along the bench so that the flaws and their corrections were instantly clear. Every now and then, he would hold up a piece and exclaim, "Ah, perfect! Exactly right." Only once, three-quarters of the way down the bench, did he pick up a piece, shake his head, and admiringly say, "I couldn't match this work myself."

A learning situation in which practise converges more on *the* practice could hardly be imagined. Yet even here the technician acknowledged one student's work as surpassing "the done thing," as exceeding the standards of established practice. Beyond that, the level of concentration and attention to detail exhibited by the students as they bent over their work could hardly be described as mindless repetition, no matter how many times they repeated a particular task. The fact that the procedures being practised will eventually become routine to them is beside the point. Paradoxically, it takes a lot of thoughtful effort to learn to do something "without thinking."

If, then, practise can exceed the limits of the practice, and drill is more often mindful than mindless, practise may nonetheless fail to make perfect in at least two ways: first, practise may be faulty; second, *the* practice may be faulty. Errors and bad habits get stamped in by practise quite as readily as proficiencies, unless the former are recognized as such and corrected. The dental technician was expert in ferreting out and diagnosing mistakes in ways that made them *evident* to the learner. In short, vigilance, not only repetition, is required to improve by practising.

Still, vigilance and care may not be enough where the practice itself is faulty. Once errors are stamped into the tradition of established practice, they often are perpetuated with great momentum. Which is to say, faulty schemas can get built in and made second nature along with, and even at times thwarting, improvements. A generation of singers in the 1930s and 1940s, enthralled by Caruso recordings, mistakenly supposed that his vocal prowess was due to great force of breath. In fact, the breathy quality of Caruso's late recordings was largely due to his declining vocal mechanism and efforts to compensate. The unhappy truth is that driving the voice by "breath congestion," as it is called, is a practice guaranteed to produce vocal "shortgevity" (Husler & Rodd-Marling, 1976, pp. 129–132).

Tradition is, of course, equally adept at perpetuating intellectual errors in textbooks and histories, such as the apocryphal story of Galileo hefting cannon balls to the top of the Leaning Tower of Pisa to test his theories (Koyré, 1937, pp. 441–453; cited in Scheffler, 1965/1985a, p. 49). Or consider the persistent notion that induction proceeds from the particular to the general, while deduction does the reverse (Skyrms, 1966, pp. 13–15). In these and other similar ways, practising and traditional practices both may fall far short of perfection.

The Social Images of Practice

Imagination plays an important role not only in practising, but also in how we think about established practice — what I shall call the "social images" of practice. Not all of them are salutary as, for example, this Elizabethan limerick:

> Multiplication is vexation,
> Division is as bad;
> The Rule of Three doth puzzle me,
> And practice drives me mad.
>
> *Anonymous manuscript, dated 1570*

I have already mentioned the popular notion of practising as bovine persistence in the face of drudgery — the idea that mere repetition is sufficient (eventually) to "get it right" and to be able to do it "without thinking."[4] While I deny that the repetition is either "mere" or sufficient for the purposes mentioned, there is a psychological truth contained in this portrait. Ironically, it has to do with the pleasures of repetition.

As one achieves a level of proficiency at various skills — for example, basic carpentry, running scales, volleying in tennis, or swimming — a rhythmic ease of execution and a sensation of fluency gradually pervades the activity. One becomes smoothly coordinated, absorbed, and focused *through* the repetitions in an almost trance-like way. Something of a balance of outgoing effort and undergoing results is achieved that is pleasing in itself. Dewey describes this sort of "integral experience" as the opposite of arrest or stasis, as a kind of "reconstruction" of experience (Dewey, 1934/1958, p. 41), and indeed it is. For the reconstruction is of one's own abilities and of the sometimes painful and frustrating experience of their exercise.

The satisfying resolution of such struggles in a fluid performance is part of the rhythmic joy of practise and in large part accounts for one's ability to keep at it. The payoff — the motivation to go on — is at least as much in the internal, *felt* balance of effort and achievement as in the achievement itself.[5]

---

[4] In *Artistry* (1982, p. 158), I called this the Penelope Theory of practise, so named after Penelope, the weaving wife of Odysseus.

[5] Here, as elsewhere, the feeling that one "knows," for example, the sensations alone of fluency and security are no reliable guide to the worth of the actual achievement.

Besides the idea of practising as repetitious drudgery, the notion of a (the) practice may carry with it a social image, perhaps several conflicting or contrasting social images, of what that practice is or ought to be. Rightly *and* wrongly, narrowly *and* broadly, certain preconceptions attach themselves to what it is to practice law or medicine, to be a musician, a violinist, even to play in a certain manner or style. "Schools" of training and instruction in painting, music, architecture, philosophy, literary criticism, science, business, and the like promote quite different conceptions of "done thing," of what is customary in the way of *the* practices to be acquired and mastered.

Michael Polanyi, for example, notes the atavistic power of certain places and institutions to promote an atmosphere of scientific apprenticeship. "The regions of Europe in which the scientific method first originated 400 years ago are scientifically still more fruitful today, in spite of their impoverishment, than several overseas areas where much more money is available for scientific research" (Polanyi, 1958, p. 53). Of course, times and traditions change, migrate (often by the immigration of a few "masters"), and get born anew in response to new demands — witness the achievements in atomic science of the Manhattan Project during World War II, or the peculiar mystique in the second half of the twentieth century of the Harvard Business School, or the IBM "corporate image," right down to sartorial style and comportment.

The fact that some of the social imagery of particular fields and occupations may turn out on closer inspection to be utter nonsense or prejudicial is beside the point. Whether or not deserved, just or unjust, accurate or misleading, inspiring or deadening, such social imagery in the arts, sciences, and professions comprises a fabric of suggestion and preconception of varying regulative force. For good or ill (and probably both), social imagery helps to shape and direct the practices within a given field: how they are seen, how they are done, and how they are taught.

The conceptual point is this: even as practising may exceed in accomplishment the limits of established practice, *the* practice is a far broader concept than practising. To take a musical example, how one plays the 'cello depends not only upon one's daily practise regimen. It depends also upon the particular tradition of 'cello instruction into which one is initiated; upon the place of the 'cello in the orchestra; upon the performance history and tradition of the instrument and its virtuosi; upon the available repertoire and acoustical properties of the instrument; even upon the physical image and posture of the player. Before the novice ever gets to a teacher, he or she is beset by all sorts of preconceptions (many of them destined to be undone, no doubt) that society reinforces willy-nilly. This aura of preconception constitutes the social practice of 'cello playing, not to be confused with the many episodes of 'cello practising under the tutelage of an instructor. A condition of learning any advanced skill is initiation into the practices of that skill *as seen from the inside,* usually by an instructor who, if not now or ever an advanced practitioner, nonetheless understands those practices from the standpoint of how they may be learned and performed.[6] That is as much a matter of learning by example as by precept and practise (for a discussion of the various roles of examples in learning, see Howard, 1982, pp. 99–112).

The Ambiguity of Practising

If by practising we mean learning by repeated trial or performance, the concept is as ambiguous as between *drill* and *training.* Certain habits, routines, and basic facilities are built up by drill to the point where, as Ryle says, one can "do them in his sleep":

> Training, on the other hand, though it embodies plenty of sheer drill, does not consist of drill. It involves the stimulation by criticism and example of the pupil's own judgment. He learns how to do things thinking what he is doing, so that every operation is itself a new lesson to him how to perform better [what Ryle calls] intelligent capacities. [He concludes,] drill dispenses with intelligence, training develops it. We do not expect the soldier to be able to read maps "in his sleep." (1949/1984, pp. 42–43)

I quite agree, except for Ryle's tag line that drill dispenses with intelligence while training develops it. Being able to do something "in one's sleep" or "without thinking about it" is an *achievement,* often the result of considerable exercise of intelligence on the part of the learner and careful intervention by an instructor. One is required to hold specific ends in view through trial after trial until errors are recognized as such and eliminated. Although routine response is the outcome, it hardly "dispenses with intelligence" in the making. In learning to play harmonic drills at the piano, for example, one must initially *think* where to place the fingers on the keyboard while reading the score.

The upshot is this: just as both training and drill are irreducible to routine response, notwithstanding the latter's *achievement* of routine response, neither is routine response entirely absent from the achievements of training in exercising critical skills of performance. Intelligence *and* routine are to be found at both ends of the practise spectrum — in drill and training — despite their different emphases and outcomes.

---

[6] Here I am using the phrase "advanced skill" as roughly synonymous with "field," "discipline," or "art form," which typically require the mastery of many subskills or facilities. For a discussion of the conceptual range and relations of skills, facilities ("techniques"), and habits, see *Artistry* (1982, pp. 176–185).

Practising and Routine

Recall now the familiar portrait of drill as the slowest, if surest, common denominator of the TIPS formula. The thoughtless routine of drill nonetheless requires discipline and direction; it isn't easy, because it's drudgery. Practising, on the other hand, requires a regimen: a set of precise exercises directed at specific ends guided by the authority of an instructor to assure that they both get done and get done well. Eventually, talent — if it is sufficient — and training — if it is rigorous enough — will win out over tedium. If not, then the potential was likely never there in the first place.

This picture of practice, particularly of drill, though not uncommon, contains a number of questionable assumptions, half truths, and plain falsehoods. Most glaring is the assumption that talent is a given, something fixed by nature and awaiting the molding process of proper instruction and diligent practising (Scheffler, 1985b, ch. 1). Suffice it to say that whatever is "given" by nature is highly volatile and changeable with time, training, and opportunity. Talent and potential, rather than explaining eventual success or failure, themselves require to be explained; they tend, in any event, to be estimated by circular reference to how well one performs en route. In effect, appeals to vague notions of talent, gifts, or potential are more like excuses or praise than explanation. Besides fixed potential, another difficulty with the TIPS formula is its reliance upon a static "technology" of fixed means to fixed ends. As Dewey reminds us, we tend rather to learn advanced skills within a *continuum* of means-ends in which the latter are mutually revisable (Dewey, 1939/1972, pp. 40–50). That is, as our competence increases, we alter not only what we do but our conceptions of what we are doing and trying to achieve. The very same exercise, for example, can have several different objectives which, as we realize them, are then seen as related to others as one facility embeds within another.

Consider, for example, what is involved in running scales on the piano. The same series of notes is repeated over and over: now for pitch accuracy, now for phraseology, now for dynamics, now for dexterity at increasing tempi, and so on. One always has an end in view, a particular achievement in mind, for which the exercise is being repeated. Each trial represents a *different* successive approximation to that end-in-view. The larger goal, of course, is to gain control of all these variables at once.

The connection of means to ends in drill, and still more in training, is similarly misrepresented in the TIPS formula by mechanical-causal analogy, as if the running off of routines *automatically* accomplished their ends. In this view, the only deficits possible are in the amount of talent and tenacity required to achieve the specified result. One fails either because one "just doesn't have it" (talent) or because one "didn't try hard enough." This view obscures the roles of intelligence, choice, and imagination in practising: intelligence in the form of growing discrimination through trial and error; choice in the form of decisions about what corrections to make; and imagination in the form of imaginal controls (like metaphor and analogy) and holding ends in view.

Drill as Thoughtful Action

Whatever else may be said about drill, it is an action, not something that "happens" to us. Writing about action in general, Israel Scheffler remarks on its "time-binding" character:

> It should not be thought mysterious that the scene of human action . . . runs both backward and forward from the immediate present. For all action links past and future, organizing or "binding" time in a characteristic way. Performed with a certain outcome in view and with further consequences anticipated, an action starts out with implicit reference to the future. But it also involves an estimate of prevailing conditions in virtue of which the action to be performed is deemed to have a good chance of succeeding. And such judgement itself, whether sound or not, purports to find its basis in past trials or past testimony. (1985b, p. 22).

As a species of action, practise — both drill and training — is similarly time-binding of past and future within a specious present.[7] That is, trial-and-error learning involves a compound of memory and anticipation in which imagination's job is to hold future ends in view and the past in review even as we prepare to take the next step. Only thus can we monitor our own progress and learn from our mistakes. And only thus can we make sense of how the rules and routines of practise connect means to ends.

As I put it elsewhere:

> Until they are enacted, how are means and ends-in-view *held*? With the possible exceptions of recipes and drill manuals, they are not simply read off from either tradition or the particular situation confronting one. Rather . . . they are held in imagination as directives (rules and routines) and frequently revised therein according to the exigencies of the situation. In effect, it is imagination that enables us to adjust our know-how to particular cases and even to revise it or transfer it to new realms of application. (Howard, 1982, p. 132)

Finally, the TIPS formula for practising entirely ignores the subtle relations among tradition, demonstration, and learning. In acquiring a practice,

---

[7] "Specious" in the sense of a present that is ever changing, of varying "width," as it were, and not literally a point psychologically in time or consciousness.

we also practise to learn it. We strive to perform it in ritualistic fashion. Put to the test, it soon becomes public what we do or do not know, can or cannot do. This sounds like worship; but not only in religious ritual is performance of the rite a demonstration that serves to pass it on to others (Scheffler, 1986, ch. 6). The rituals of art, science, technology, and education have a similar function. Practising their rituals simultaneously exemplifies *the* practices of those fields and becomes a way for others to learn them — and to surpass them.

Accordingly, we may distinguish the cross-sectional, "synchronic" instructional payoff of practising particular facilities from the longitudinal, "diachronic" payoff of traditional practices. The latter teach across historical time, as it were, from one generation to the next. The former are more a matter of identifying *with* the practices of a given field or discipline, of taking them into oneself, of mastering them for the sake of competency. That is very like a process of initiation into a tradition by aspiration, demonstration, and precept.

We cannot escape the traditional demands of our chosen disciplines or professions, however much we may eventually depart from them. We grow into them precisely in order to grow beyond them and maybe alter them for future generations. Yet none of this personal and historical drama of learning is captured in the simplistic notion of drill as drudgery (nor in the equally simplistic assimilation of training to drill). Drill, on the contrary, is one of the most powerful, intelligent, imaginative means of learning at our disposal, enabling us to master the facilities required by advanced skills. By way of drill we not only learn by example and instruction, but also become examples of the very things we learn. One might even think of this as the existential predicament of practising anything at all: you are what you learn to do routinely.

References

Bruner, J. S. (1986). *Actual minds, possible worlds.* Cambridge, MA: Harvard University Press.

Dewey, J. (1958). *Art as experience.* New York: Putnam. (Original work published 1934)

Dewey, J. (1972). *Theory of valuation.* Chicago: University of Chicago Press. (Original work published 1939)

Howard, V. A. (1982). *Artistry: The work of artists.* Indianapolis: Hackett.

Howard, V. A. (1992). *Learning by all means: Lessons from the arts.* New York: Peter Lang.

Husler, F., & Rodd-Marling, Y. (1976). *Singing, the physical nature of the vocal organ.* London: Hutchinson.

Jensen, A. R. (1972). *Genetics and education.* London: Methuen.

Jensen, A. R. (1981). *Straight talk about mental tests.* New York: Free Press.

Kagan, J., & Brim, O. G., Jr. (Eds.). (1980). *Constancy and change in human development.* Cambridge, MA: Harvard University Press.

Koyré, A. (1937). Galilée et l'expérience de pise. *Annales de l'Université de Paris,* pp. 441–453.

Polanyi, M. (1958). *Personal knowledge: Towards a post-critical philosophy.* London: Routledge & Kegan Paul.

Ryle, G. (1984). *The concept of mind.* Chicago: University of Chicago Press. (Original work published 1949)

Seashore, C. E. (1947). *In search of beauty in music: A scientific approach to musical aesthetics.* New York: Ronald Press.

Scheffler, I. (1985a). *Conditions of knowledge.* Chicago: University of Chicago Press. (Original work published 1965)

Scheffler, I. (1985b). *Of human potential.* London: Routledge & Kegan Paul.

Scheffler, I. (1986). *Inquiries, philosophical studies of language, science, and learning.* Indianapolis: Hackett.

Skinner, B. F. (1965). *Science and human behavior.* New York: Free Press.

Skyrms, B. (1966). *Choice and chance: An introduction to inductive logic.* Belmont, MA: Dickenson.

Essay Review

Progressive Journeying

KATHLEEN MURPHEY

GARY DeCOKER

To Open Minds: Chinese Clues to the Dilemma of Contemporary Education
by Howard Gardner.
New York: Basic Books, 1989. 326 pp. $21.95, $14.95 (paper).

In his most recent book, *To Open Minds: Chinese Clues to the Dilemma of Contemporary Education,* Howard Gardner travels to China where he applies his theories of creativity:

> As a developmental psychologist, I held views about the optimal sequence of artistic development in early childhood — exploration first, skill development later; these views were directly challenged by the precocious yet flexible mastery of styles and forms exhibited by many young Chinese children. As a student of the arts, I embraced the prevalent Western concept of the arts as cognitive, problem-finding, world-remaking activities; these views were challenged by the Chinese belief in artistic activity as the re-creation of traditional beautiful forms and the engendering of moral behavior. As a researcher in education, I was persuaded of the importance of various "progressive ideas," and yet saw the Chinese achieve spectacular results by defying the very precepts I cherished. (p. 14)

The book, however, is less about China than about Gardner's own intellectual explorations. Rather than exploring Chinese history and contemporary society from within, he uses China as a challenge to his own theories, a strategy with both positive and negative results. Gardner's thinking focuses on the U.S. debate

Harvard Educational Review   Vol. 61   No. 2   May 1991

between traditional and progressive educational philosophies, which becomes the central construct for the entire book. China itself is secondary, relevant only when it offers insight into this debate.

Much like late nineteenth-century travelogues, we learn more about the author of *To Open Minds* than the country he explored. The authors of these travelogues often gave Europe and the United States their first look at distant cultures. Although today these writings appear naive, self-centered, and ethnocentric, we excuse the authors, thankful for their documentation of a bygone era. Contemporary anthropologists, working in a field that traces its origins to these early travelogues, have evolved methods that attempt to balance the subjective and the objective by exploring the culture of study on its own terms, rather than on those of the researcher.

Gardner forgoes the anthropologists' caution. Instead, he chooses the travelogue approach, which centers on his own thinking and the intellectual questions of his own culture. Unlike the early travelogues, however, Gardner self-consciously discusses his method and his purpose. Before the book even begins, he states in a two-paragraph note written at the time of publication: "In *To Open Minds,* I probe my experiences in China for clues to the resolution of a struggle within American education — the clash between progressive and traditional forces which has intensified over the last few decades" (p. x). At the book's end, he again reminds us that he remains "interested more in the implications of these observations for Western attitudes and actions in the educational realm than in the conduct of sinological anthropology for its own sake" (p. 257).

Gardner's self-conscious autobiographical approach stems from his observation that visitors to China often have unpredictable reactions to Chinese culture and practices. Gardner concludes that these reactions seem

> directly to reflect each witness's personal value system: his or her own education, relations to authority, attitudes about children, aesthetic standards, and overall view of human nature. As one might put it in an American idiom, individuals' reactions to what they saw in Chinese classrooms and across hotel lobbies revealed "where they were coming from."
>
> And so I became convinced that there was a crucial dimension to the arguments I wished to put forth about creativity, culture, education, and China: that is, the autobiographical part. (p. 15)

Thus, moving through time and between cultures, Gardner takes the reader on an autobiographical journey of insights and experiences that document the evolution of his thinking about the progressive versus traditional education debate.[1] Within this debate, on U.S. intellectual soil, Gardner educates and convinces the reader of the value of his exploration. Indeed, the book becomes an example of the open-ended exploring that he advocates. Part One of the book, Gardner's autobiographical chapters, brings a freshness, spontaneity, and sincerity to a philosophical debate that is often couched in more abstract, less

---

[1] Gardner discusses the progressive (student-centered, process-oriented) and traditional (teacher-centered, product-oriented) approaches in the Prologue.

accessible terms. In Parts Two and Three, where Gardner comments on China, his approach leads to some problems, which we will discuss later.

Gardner's journey takes the reader from his childhood home, to his intellectual flowering as an undergraduate at Harvard, to his mentors around the world, to his research projects in Cambridge and Boston, to China several times, and then home again. He travels to China first as a member and then as a leader of U.S. delegations; later, on a more extended visit accompanied by his wife and eighteen-month-old son, he conducts research.

In this travelogue with a philosophic agenda, Gardner puts aside the language of a philosopher and assumes the personal voice of a seeker, a voice that speaks to an audience beyond the world of academics. His autobiographical approach, an unusual and refreshing way of engaging in educational debate, and his willingness to write so personally will appeal especially to teachers who seek a broader perspective for themselves. Readers will reflect on their own intellectual and social growth as they follow Gardner's saga. Harvard graduates will recognize a shared graduate or undergraduate world; China travelers will rediscover China through an educator's eyes.

By comparing the interplay of theory and practice in Chinese and U.S. art education, Gardner is able to refine his thinking on creativity. In academic subjects, logical-mathematical thinking is usually considered the dominant supporting skill. As Gardner asserts in his research on creativity, however, people have "multiple intelligences," although intelligences in the arts often are not identified or valued. Gardner's theory of multiple intelligences "stresses the different abilities and sets of abilities found among children and the need for youngsters to have opportunities to find and develop their talents" (p. 290).[2] The developing of these abilities, especially in the arts, requires practice. Gardner's observations of art instruction in the two cultures, therefore, present concrete examples of the differences between the traditional and progressive philosophies.

Gardner's interdisciplinary research background gives him a strong academic base for carrying out such a comparison. He draws on his self-described "marginal" relationship to several academic disciplines, as well as his early training in music. Gardner's own "multiple intelligences" make him a sophisticated generalist who breathes new life into an old debate. Because of the boundaries between academic disciplines, most researchers are not in the position to undertake such a study, much less to see the questions he asks as being so central to education in the United States today.

The passion that Gardner displays for his work is striking. He presents his early schooling and years at Harvard, focusing on the process of his intellectual growth. Each event unfolds into the next, eventually leading into the present and a new series of hypotheses. Where these hypotheses will lead is a mystery even to Gardner. The lack of finality, although somewhat unsatisfying, is also comforting. Gardner reminds us that the struggle to achieve meaning will never end. His description of human pursuits demonstrates that the quest for certainty

---

[2] Gardner refers the reader to his *Frames of Mind: The Theory of Multiple Intelligences* (New York: Basic Books, 1983) for a more detailed discussion of his theory of human intelligences.

is eternal, but that certainty itself is never final. This is a lesson often lost in an educational system with clearly marked endings from preschool through the doctorate. Gardner himself, as he struggled for a specific research focus during his graduate school years, would have been reassured by such a lesson.

On another level, however, Gardner is succumbing to the need for certainty, which is a weakness when he visits China. He presents ideas, such as his definition of creativity or his approach to art education, and then tends to evaluate the Chinese in relation to them. Sometimes he seems to have crossed the Pacific to convert rather than to understand. This approach leads to many unresolved confrontations with Chinese educators, often leaving Gardner frustrated. After a lengthy discussion about the relationship of art to morality, Gardner states, "My Chinese colleagues listened to these queries, and some even tried to answer them, but I received the unambiguous impression that my remarks were considered beside the point" (p. 267). Instead of continually confronting the Chinese with his own intellectual concerns, Gardner might have presented his hosts with more opportunities to explain themselves on their own terms. Chinese voices are lost in Gardner's narrative.

In fact, as Gardner travels in China, he needs, perhaps, some of the anthropologist's caution he has cast aside. At times Gardner reverses his initial purpose of using China to gain insight into U.S. education and uses the U.S. debate as a construct to understand China. This, too, is apparent in the note that precedes the book. Referring to unrest in China during the spring of 1989, he states, "I did not anticipate that an analogous but even more far-reaching struggle between progressive and traditional forces would soon be played out on the streets of China" (p. x). The issues of Tiananmen Square, however, certainly require a more complex analytical framework, one that makes use of social science theories and includes a historical perspective on China.

Because of the power that Gardner's personal history brings to his narrative, it is also somewhat surprising that he chooses not to explore the historical dimensions of Chinese education more thoroughly. Needless to say, there are countless echoes of past Chinese eras in the present philosophy and practice of education in China. The current system of education is, however, very different from the civil servant examination system of a hundred years ago. The content and availability of education have changed radically. While China may, indeed, come up short when measured against U.S. progressive educational methods, it might fare differently if measured against other criteria that take into consideration China's educational goals, its resources, and its own long history. As this lack of attention to Chinese educational history shows, Gardner's creative exploring, when taken beyond the academic areas that are his strengths, sometimes lacks rigor, the very weakness that traditionalists emphasize most in their criticism of progressive education. Gardner speaks to this issue toward the end of the book:

> By no means — and by no stretch — am I an expert on China. My background reading about China has been scattered and unsystematic. Even if my analysis should obtain about contemporary Communist China,

I have no way of establishing which of the features are peculiar to that society; which would be found in any twentieth-century Chinese community; and which date back to earlier times. . . . I do believe, however, that my conclusions are similar to those that would be reached by others from my general background and orientation — including many readers of this book. (p. 257)

When guided by his creativity, however, Gardner uses his experiences to bring focus to the basic differences between the two cultures. An incident involving his son's attempt to put a key in the narrow opening of a box in a Chinese hotel, and Chinese observers' reaction to it, vividly demonstrates Gardner's point about child-rearing. The Chinese observers were anxious to guide the child's unpracticed hand so he would quickly, quietly, and aesthetically achieve success (pp. 3–6). Gardner and his wife, however, considered their son's noisy exploratory behavior valuable in itself; they were not concerned about the immediate result of his behavior but rather the process of his learning. According to Gardner:

The incident with the key helped me to gain a firmer grasp on a major tension that has long pervaded discussions about both education *and* creativity. There is, on the one hand, the need to develop the "basic skills" and the "core knowledge" upon which mature achievements in a field must be based; in contrast, there is the appeal of a "hands-off," nondirective, and progressive educational philosophy, which seems distinctly preferable if creativity is to be fostered in young children and fully realized in later years. China and the United States turn out to embrace two radically different solutions to the dilemma of creativity versus basic skills. (p. 7)

Gardner enriches his autobiographical journey with general cultural impressions of China. His views, however, sometimes seem unnecessarily harsh. As he expresses frustration and anger at being given separate, better dining arrangements than his Chinese hosts (p. 130), at being caught in competition between these hosts (p. 194), at being overprotected from the rigors of Chinese life while traveling (p. 131) or at being swept into a crowd while waiting for a bus (pp. 213–214), we are reminded more of a first-time visitor to China than of a thoughtful academic with a philosophic mission. While Gardner understands, for example, some of the practical reasons for the separation of Westerners at mealtime, he nonetheless comes to the conclusion "that, as a group, the Chinese tend to be ethnocentric, xenophobic, and racist" (p. 130). His negative reactions to his daily experiences in China show more of his immediate frustration than careful reflection about a foreign culture. More rigorous digging by Gardner for the reasons behind things he observed, or more acknowledgement that there could be a cultural or historical reason for something he perceived as irrational, would help dispel the impression that he is sometimes too quick to use casual experiences in China, both good and bad, to support his emerging educational hypotheses.

Gardner, like many other Westerners, finds it easiest to like and know those Chinese who are the most elite intellectually and who have been trained in

Western countries — people who remind Gardner of former premier Chou Enlai. Gardner describes one such person as "an altogether charming host, easy to talk to, representative of those infinitely gracious and knowledgeable elder leaders who delight the fortunate visitor to China" (p. 129). The Western-trained, Western-sympathetic intelligentsia in China understand and reflect Western values, style, and thinking. They also speak English. Such scholars represent a long tradition of Chinese history, but they are few in number. They are, in effect, as marginal and elite relative to their own society and professions as Gardner is to his. That other Chinese people with less training, less status, and little skill in Western diplomacy and conversational style should be harder for Gardner to appreciate, especially in formal meetings, should come as no surprise. After one strained formal dinner with little conversation, Gardner concludes that he and his U.S. colleagues "were, in fact, dealing with a problem intrinsic to China today and, quite possibly, to China through the ages: that is, except for a few major leaders who happen also to be extroverts, Chinese adults are awkward with foreigners" (p. 128). These encounters with the Chinese could have provoked Gardner to further reflection on Chinese culture and his relationship to it, rather than to such strongly worded generalizations.

Gardner's observations of Chinese classrooms brought other challenges. He often describes his frustration at being shown "canned" demonstrations of students performing well-rehearsed music or copying model artwork. To get around this, he devised what he calls the "minor inspiration" of requesting that students draw objects they had never seen before — a group of ten-year-olds drew his face (p. 183), and kindergarten students drew his son's Western-style stroller (pp. 244–245). These demonstrations allowed Gardner to see for himself the creative ability of the young Chinese. "I had found out what I wanted: Chinese children are not simply tied to schemas; they can depart to some extent from a formula when so requested" (p. 183). This approach, however, seemed less important to Gardner's Chinese hosts. Unrehearsed drawings may have represented artistic ability to Gardner, but in China quality is revealed in the following of a series of steps leading to mastery. To the Chinese, well-rehearsed demonstrations most clearly illustrate the accomplishments of the students and teacher.

A similar conflict over the definition of quality arose when Gardner gave a tour of U.S. schools to a group of Chinese educators. He, too, carefully chose the programs: model schools, avant-garde music, and highly abstract artwork. At one school, students were given a pile of newspapers and told to make the highest structure possible, an activity that some of the Chinese were unable to value (p. 169). These experiences lead Gardner to conclude thoughtfully that "it is simply not enough to expose Chinese to abstract art and to tell them to get used to it; one must help them understand the aesthetic, cultural, and historical milieu in which it arose and the personal and aesthetic needs it fulfills" (p. 169). Thus, on his own soil, Gardner seems to see more clearly the complexity of understanding a different system of values.

In the end, however, Gardner refuses to give up his support for the progressive model. When advocating greater support for art education in the United

States, he uses progressive values such as creativity and problem solving, even though he also comments on the difficulty of using the progressive model with anything but superior teachers, students, and schools. When Gardner visited art programs in the United States, he found:

> Many places had only skeletal programs, staffed by people who neither knew nor cared about the arts. Because few teachers had artistic skills, and because those who did were skittish about exposing their works to students, the chief activity was simply giving children opportunities to paint, to pot, or to dance. This ploy was fine during the early years of childhood but made little sense in middle childhood and preadolescence when youngsters crave skills. The resulting works were either derivative from the mass media, or showed a vestige of a good idea but lacked the technical means to express it properly. In my terms, a creative spark, but no basic skills. (p. 141)

Given these limitations, the Chinese approach of following a prescribed series of basic skill lessons might make it possible to offer art to a wider audience of school children. Indeed, the major difference between the two countries may be, as Gardner himself notes (p. 250), the Chinese satisfaction with a uniform, if unexceptional, art curriculum versus the American striving for superior art programs in an atmosphere where most programs are "bleak" (p. 141).

When Gardner does make recommendations for U.S. education based on the Chinese model, he brings back insights that are apt to appeal to the traditional U.S. educational establishment. The Chinese tradition of fostering disciplined social skills suggests to Gardner that U.S. schooling might stress "civility":

> From an early age, children should learn how to behave at home, in school, and with others — how to be polite, to share, to listen, to follow reasonable instructions, to proceed by working things out rather than by intrusive acts. Such civility is essential if education is to be effective at later years. While children ought to be free to explore the range of materials flexibly, there is no need for them to do so in ways that are disruptive to others or injurious to themselves. (p. 299)

Whether one agrees with this or not, it represents a welcome attempt by Gardner to understand and learn from the Chinese approach to art education.

Gardner explains that in China "there is widespread consensus on the importance of arts education and the desirability of teaching the major art forms in the same step-by-step fashion to all children." Arts education, he adds, is widely seen as a factor in developing good citizenship (p. 220). This is, according to Gardner, in sharp contrast to the United States:

> The powers that be in America have, for the most part, ignored education in the arts. Unlike the Chinese and certain other Asian and European populations, our nation does not have a long tradition of cherishing artistic performance in our young. Nor do we expect leaders of our country to be conversant with different art forms. (p. 139)

In his concluding remarks, Gardner acknowledges how much his experiences in China have prodded his thinking. "My time in China stimulated me to come to grips with my own beliefs about creativity and, more broadly, to rethink my views about education" (p. 288). The many "opposing sets of values" Gardner observes force him to grapple anew with old challenges:

> With respect to education as well, I found myself increasingly pressed to reconcile opposing sets of values: a respect for tradition, as compared with a dedication to the understanding of new ideas and forms; a concentration on the development of basic skills, as opposed to an encouragement of free and untrammeled exploration; the desirability of attaining full mastery in one domain of practice, as opposed to the pursuit of a broad-based liberal arts education that provides at least a nodding familiarity with the full range of established domains of knowledge. To be sure, I had been aware of these antinomies before, but the China experience (in conjunction with the fresh debates at home, even on my own university campus) brought these issues to a head. (p. 289)

Having defined these pairs of opposites, Gardner rejects a compromise that suggests following one side while keeping the other approach in mind: "Yet I am not satisfied with the simple compromise that either approach will do" (p. 298). Here we might expect a Deweyan reconciliation. Instead, Gardner refers to Whitehead's "rhythmic claims of freedom and discipline" to present an idea he calls "individual-centered schooling" that moves back and forth between the American and Chinese approaches, guided by the needs of the developing child. From China, Gardner borrows what most impressed him — classroom environments that reminded him of traditional apprenticeships where children concentrate on long-term tasks:

> But China reminded me as well of certain educational virtues often lost sight of in our own country but still happily manifest in that more traditional society. I saw children from an early age deeply involved in and excited by activities of learning — both in the scholastic curriculum and in artistic and other performance domains. Without apparent prodding, students as young as six or seven would willingly work for an hour or more on their paintings, their calligraphy, their sums, or their constructions. They would return to these activities day after day, gaining genuine skills in the process, so that by late childhood, they would already have achieved considerable mastery. They were neither proud nor boastful so far as I could see, but rather gained pleasure from what they were doing. (p. 292)

Gardner's "individual-centered schooling" extends some of his earlier work by proposing a creative, exploratory period up to the age of about seven, after which the child would enter an apprenticeship stage until roughly age fourteen. During the second stage the child would focus on skill building and learning from a master "in at least three areas: an art form or craft, a form of bodily discipline (such as dance or sport), and an academic discipline (such as history, general science)" (p. 300). The apprenticeship stage in particular grows out of Gardner's positive impression of Chinese children concentrating on tasks in ways not generally expected or demanded in the United States. This stage seems to be an especially interesting blend of the concerns of a developmental psychologist, a student of China, and a progressive. Then, in the third period, about age fourteen to twenty-one, the child would build on the skills learned, but in a more exploratory, questioning, and creative way. Gardner also proposes this three-stage system — moving from progressive to traditional and back to progressive — for Chinese education, a task he leaves for the Chinese to adapt in their own way.

To Open Minds does present us with some "Chinese Clues to the Dilemma of Contemporary Education," but, more importantly, it presents us with a progressive experiment that demonstrates how minds, our minds, can be enriched by entering Gardner's intellectual world as he travels to another culture. Through the gentle back-door of a travelogue we are pulled into one of the major educational debates of our century. We are especially inspired by the strength of his progressive voice, which becomes clearer through his China experience. Such voices have been all too infrequent in this past decade, drowned out by essentialists and economic pragmatists who too often have had the last word in educational policy matters. We also applaud his efforts to synthesize his research and study by proposing a new model of education.

The weakness of the book relates to the weakness of the progressive philosophy itself. How often have its critics noted that, in the rush to be creative, progressives have neglected basic skills. Here we note Gardner's lack of depth in his cultural and historical knowledge of China. By being a novice in matters Chinese, Gardner runs the risk of describing and reacting to what may be only a caricature of China and Chinese education, a caricature that may close rather than open his readers' minds to further study of Chinese education and the real challenges it presents to U.S. educators. A second weakness is Gardner's failure to follow Dewey's warning against an either/or philosophy; overemphasis on pinning things down into predetermined categories can defeat the purpose of learning. Thus, in the end, Gardner was unable to prevent his own philosophy from restricting his imaginative construct of journeying to another country to find clues to educational dilemmas at home. In the end, he and his readers were unable to learn as much from China as they might have.

Nonetheless, with those concerns in mind, this book sets it own norms and lives up to them. Readers will learn from Gardner's intellectual and cross-cultural experiences as they become part of the progressive experiment his life and work exemplify. In true progressive style, Gardner raises questions and leaves others the task of constructing answers with him. His work, presented in this accessible form, thrusts a debate usually viewed as internal to the United States into the international arena where it belongs. We praise Gardner's attempt to intersect the interdisciplinary, cross-cultural, and personal, and we hope other researchers will search as ambitiously as he has for "clues to the dilemmas of contemporary education."

Book Review

MARIE F. McCARTHY

Music, Mind, and Education
by Keith Swanwick.
New York: Routledge, 1988. 169 pp. $49.95, $16.95 (paper).

In *Music, Mind, and Education,* Keith Swanwick forwards a theory for music education in Britain. Following in the tradition of Karl Popper (1972), Swanwick
believes that "celebration and refutation of theories is the central activity of both
the sciences and the humanities" (p. 7). The author not only presents a vital
and provocative theory of music education, but also orchestrates his composition
so that theoretical arguments exposed in the first five chapters are subsequently
used to explore "three areas of practical difficulty and decision making in music
education" (p. 89): the structure of a music curriculum, the cultural context,
and the assessment of student progress.

   The overall significance of this book may be identified from multiple vantage
points. It represents a synthesis of the philosophy and research of Britain's first
professor of music education; moreover, it contributes to the corpus of British
publications of the last two decades dealing specifically with the relationship
between music in society and music in education. I refer in particular to Christopher Small's *Music, Society, Education* (1977), Peter Fletcher's *Education and
Music* (1987), and Lucy Green's *Music on Deaf Ears: Musical Meaning, Ideology,
Education* (1988).[1]

---

[1] In addition, the *British Journal of Sociology of Education* provided a forum for a lively discourse
between Keith Swanwick, Graham Vulliamy, and John Shepherd on the sociology of music education
(Vol. 5, No. 1, 1984, pp. 49–56, 57–76; Vol. 5, No. 3, 1984, pp. 303 –307; Vol. 6, No. 2, 1985, pp.
225–229). It is curious that a similar corpus of literature dealing at a global level with the relationship
of music, society, and education has not emerged in the United States. Instead, publications have
tended to be focused on one specific domain of music education — philosophy, psychology, or
curriculum, for example. This trend may be interpreted as reflecting the prevalence of specialization
within the discipline of music education in this country.

Harvard Educational Review   Vol. 61 No. 1   February 1991

Within the global, tripartite domain of music, mind, and education, Swanwick probes issues related to the philosophy of music, the psychology of musical experience, and the sociology and curriculum of music education. The book's scope, therefore, is extensive, and the content is densely textured and carefully sequenced within its 155 pages. Some of the most striking and valuable features are 1) the progressive and coherent model that Swanwick offers for exploring musical development; 2) the practical questions he poses regarding the potential of music in public school settings; 3) criticisms he forwards about the nature of research into musical development, the dominance of behavioral objectives in music pedagogy, and the conceptual approach to music teaching and learning; and 4) the creative integration of theories and principles drawn from the philosophy, psychology, and sociology of the arts, from education, and music education in particular.

The purpose of this review is threefold: to outline the foundations of Swanwick's theory, to assess its curricular implications, and to attempt a comparative view of music education in Britain and in the United States.

Theoretical Foundations

Swanwick prefaces the book's arguments by reestablishing the need for theory in music education. We must take theorizing seriously in our profession, he claims. Based on research he directed in Britain between 1985 and 1987, the author concludes that music education there is founded on three central and contrasting "pillars": a theory that emphasizes the transmission of traditional musical values and practices (e.g., the Kodaly method, or music examination boards that are scattered throughout the Western world and in British colonies); a child-centered theory (e.g., the Orff approach, or the orientation of the U.S. publication, *The Manhattanville Music Curriculum Program* [*MMCP*]); and a third, more recent theory focused on developing in students a respect for alternative musical traditions that are alternatives to those recognized in the first theory. Subsequently, Swanwick sets out to examine the underlying assumptions of each theory, "its 'history' and value system" (p. 17), and to bring together those ideas that seem most valuable to contemporary music education.

Swanwick's view of human musicality belongs clearly to the cognitivist approach: "music works through minds" (p. 4). His ideas, however, embrace a broader spectrum than does much research in the psychology of music education. In fact, he openly criticizes this type of research for lacking a sense of direction, for being waylaid by behaviorism and other psychological fashions, and for its narrow definition of musical ability as reflected by tests of musical measurement (p. 4). Rather than focus exclusively on the psycho-acoustical properties of sound (pitch, loudness, rhythm, and timbre), which the author claims have had a considerable effect on the formulation of music curricula in North America, he perceives music to be "interesting sounds as expressive gestures embodied in coherent forms" (p. 24). Swanwick builds a spiral model of musical experience and development based on these sensory, expressive, and structural elements of music (see figure).

126

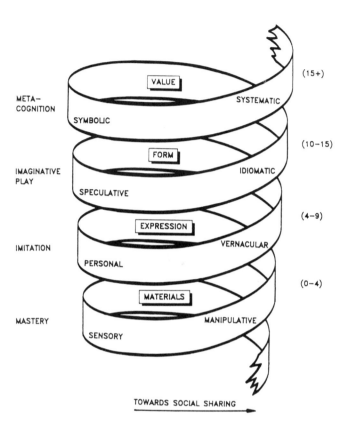

Towards social sharing

The spiral of musical development

Originally published in "The Sequence of Musical Development: A Study of Children's Composition," by Keith Swanwick and June Tillman, *British Journal of Music Education*, *3* (November 1986), copyright © Cambridge University Press.

The eight transformations, or "developmental modes," are illuminated by drawing on a theory of play in human development, outlined on the left side of the spiral. A child proceeds from gaining mastery and control over musical sounds, to identifying with the expressive features of music and its structural and stylistic norms, to developing the ability to reflect on and evaluate music and musical experience. Inherent in this model is the constant interplay between music as a personal, subjective, and exploratory experience (left side of spiral), to one that is communal, conventional, and focused on socially shared knowledge (right side).

Swanwick and Tillman's model of musical development is carefully structured, richly contextualized, and elicits many questions for further exploration. At a glance, the spiral transmits the notion that, for example, the capacity to reflect on music and musical values belongs to the final developmental mode. His placement of "value" here in a narrowly defined domain of metacognition limits its meaning in a music-education context. It does not address or include the more general use of the term in relation to the development of students' musical and stylistic preferences, something that occurs much earlier than fifteen years of age. Whatever its shortcomings, the model is one worthy of examination and reflection by music educators, for a variety of reasons: 1) it is founded on a developmental theory of play that is intrinsically related to artistic growth; 2) the eight developmental modes that constitute the spiral present a logical, sequential, and credible explanation of musical development; 3) these modes clarify the "deep dialectic process" between personal and social engagement in music at various developmental levels; 4) the model breaks from the traditional quantitative (concepts/skills) approach to musical development and focuses on the qualitative (transformations) nature of growth patterns, and, thus, has the potential to open up new discourse on artistic development; 5) language used to develop the model is accessible and "vernacular," to borrow one such term.

At a generic level, the author focuses on two interwoven themes — the nature of musical experience and its implications for education and human growth, and the manner in which individuals construct their worlds through the arts and especially through music. In order to focus the development of those themes, Swanwick poses keen questions throughout the book that contribute immeasurably to the book's cohesive, unified impact. For example: What is it that makes music musical? What is the unique function of music in education? What are the "central pillars" of contemporary music education? Can the diversity of world music be brought into the classroom? If so, in what form? Are music classrooms conducive to eliciting significant musical encounters? How can musical progress be assessed?

The solutions provided by Swanwick for these and other questions will be synthesized in this review by addressing two relationships between his theory and his practical suggestions for music education: first, the relationship between the author's worldview of music and his approach to world musics in education, and second, the implications of his theory of artistic growth and experience for curriculum development in music.

World Musics in Education

Every theory of music education is founded on and structured around a worldview of music. By "worldview" I refer to an individual's perception of the nature and role of music in the development of the human species. From the outset, Swanwick acknowledges the influence of Karl Popper's theory of objective knowledge in framing his philosophy of music. In this theory, Popper envisages a tripartite world; the first is the physical world of objects and events, the second is the world of mental states or subjective experience, and the third ("World Three") is the world of theories or ideas in the objective sense (p. 7; see also Popper, 1972, p. 154). Consonant with this theory, music is placed in "World

Three," an autonomous world of ideas that may take the form of "scientific theories, philosophical reasonings, musical works, paintings, novels, poems, and so on" (p. 7). Recognition of this epistemological underpinning is crucial to understanding and assessing Swanwick's theory of music education.

According to this theory, musical works and their inherent musical procedures represent the primary source of meaning, since these "*products . . . enable us to communicate with one another*" (p. 14). Such products are motivated by the human biological and psychological necessity to symbolize, thus identifying music as central to the development of "mind."

The reader is guided well into the theory before the author defines "mind" as comprising "the great networks of symbolic processes that human cultures have generated, sustained, and refined through the ages" (pp. 104–105). These "great networks" are not clearly identified. If one assumes that the author is referring to symbolic processes such as language, art, music, theater, and myth, then he subsequently fails to acknowledge the interrelatedness and interdependence of these various networks of symbolic processes in any given culture. This becomes evident when his theory is applied to practice.

The implications of this worldview for music education are manifold. If, as Clifford Geertz succinctly expresses, "art and the equipment to grasp it are made in the same shop" (1983, p. 118), then the author needs to clarify the distinction between the *universality* of the necessity to symbolize and the *particularity* of the manifestation of that necessity in various cultures. Translated into Geertz's metaphor, while the equipment to create and respond to art is universal, the equipment to grasp it — that is, to interpret its symbolic processes — is embedded in the myths and beliefs of cultural and subcultural groups. Jerome Bruner's contrast of the humanities and the sciences highlights the futility of aspiring, as Swanwick advocates, toward self and cultural transcendence by abstracting and isolating "sets of sound" from their cultural contexts. Humanities achieve universality through "context sensitivity, a work of science through context independence" (1986, p. 50).

In the absence of this distinction in music education, the multiple layers of social and cultural meaning in music are likely to be neglected to the exclusive consideration of musical products as universal "objects" of communication. Furthermore, the "complexity within simplicity," a feature endemic to many world musics, may be misinterpreted or lost in the process of isolating the music from its cultural meaning.[2] How, then, does the author deal with multicultural musics in education?

Swanwick's basic assumptions about the role of music in culture determine his approach to world musics in education. With regard to formal music education, he assumes a firm stance against presenting musics with their cultural labels, prejudices, and stereotypes. Instead, he maintains, the focus of instruction ought to be on the phenomena and musical procedures that are relatively inde-

---

[2] This concept is borrowed from Ellis (1987).

129

pendent of cultural ownership. Only after the music has really been experienced should cultural values be introduced. Musical genres that have become "emotionally embroiled in local cultural practices and fads" (p. 101) have no place in the curriculum, at least until the "territorial origins" of the genre lose their significance.

While the author's consideration of ethical issues such as cultural stereotyping and building an intercultural attitude are commendable, his suggestions for presenting world musics in the classroom reduce the potential of music as a cultural subject in the curriculum. In an effort to overcome the "impediments" caused by "new sounds," "alien expressive character," and "difficult structure," Swanwick seeks to extract and abstract the "music" from its social context and simply transcend the very cultural conditions that cause the impediments in the first place. For example, he takes the pentatonic scale and, by working through the developmental spiral, illustrates how children would progress from a sensory response to the "sets of sound" to recognizing it in music "from China to Scotland" (p. 116). While this progression is acceptable and logical, does it necessarily maintain the integrity of music as an intercultural art form and the uniqueness of music in various cultural contexts? David Elliott warns of this reductionist approach to music as culture: "It is not sufficient to pick the fruits of a culture, one must also look to its roots and shoots" (1990, p. 151).

The author's approach to any world music through experience with its musical procedures is educationally laudable. However, he overemphasizes the common elements of music across cultures, thus transmitting to the students the "similarities that bind" to the possible neglect of the "differences that distinguish us as subsets of the human species" (Anderson & Campbell, 1989, p. viii). In his recent publication, *Musical Beliefs: Psychological, Mythical, and Educational Perspectives* (1990), Robert Walker offers a two-tier approach to multicultural music education that takes Swanwick's theory one crucial step further. In Walker's approach, students progress from experiences with "culture-free sounds" (similar to Swanwick's "sets of sound") to experiences with the cultural sounds of music in the context of their belief systems (1990, pp. 222–223).

That Swanwick criticizes the use of the conceptual approach to music education is curious and inconsistent with the above support for universals in music. In his opinion, concepts are at best "critical generalizations" (p. 146). In lieu of concepts, he focuses on "features" of music that strike us "with what is unique" to the musical context. Applied to the introduction of world musics in education, the focus is foremost on the uniqueness of music in a particular context and not, as advocated earlier in the book, on its abstraction from that context.

The Arts as "Different": Implications for Curriculum Development

Perhaps the most valuable contribution Swanwick makes is his theory of artistic growth and the spiral model that articulates that theory. He chose a spiral curriculum for several reasons. Like musical development, it is cyclical and cumulative. It can also represent the dialectical relationship between individual and social responses to music. A significant feature of this model is his nontraditional application of Jean Piaget's ideas to music education. In lieu of founding his theory on Piaget's developmental stage theory, Swanwick draws on his developmental theory of play (1951/1962). This choice is consonant with the author's general dissatisfaction with the prevalent atomistic view of how individuals perceive music. He presents an alternative perspective based on the notion of man as *homo ludens,* man the play-maker.

Mastery, imitation, and imaginative play comprise the developmental transformations of Piaget's theory of play. Swanwick offers analogous musical elements for these processes — control of sound materials, identification with expressive character, and recognition and formation of structural relationships in music. He also argues for strong associations between them and the three major modes of participating in music — mastery in performing, imitation in listening, and imaginative play in "forming" or creating.

Evolving out of this tri-angled framework, and augmented by a fourth aspect of metacognition, the author builds the spiral of musical development already illustrated. The fundamental thrust of Swanwick's model is the uniqueness of the artistic mode of experience. Therefore, the discipline of music in public schools needs to be founded, structured, and assessed in ways different from nonartistic disciplines. While Swanwick is not the first to make this distinction, he furthers the discourse by highlighting effectively 1) the futility of applying models from other curricular disciplines to music, and 2) the acute need for a new theory for the arts in education. What novel ideas does he contribute toward this new theory?

First, the author defines the function of music in education and the function of education in musical development. A rather debatable equation is drawn between "musical instruction" as a feature of schools and "musical encounters" as a feature of enculturative settings where people learn "simply by being there" (p. 117). Ultimate experiences in the arts, Swanwick claims, can be experienced more easily outside the classroom. Since the aim of education is perceived as the development of mind, music instruction thus revolves around musical criticism and musical analysis. In this way, schools function as laboratories for developing in the students "a state of readiness" for engaging in meaningful musical encounters "out there," in everyday life. Such polarization of "musical instruction" and "musical encounters" is reductionist, and it creates an unnatural separation between the worlds of school music and community music.

At one level, Swanwick's notion of educating toward "a state of readiness" for musical encounters may be compared to the aim of general music education articulated by U.S. music education philosopher Bennett Reimer: to develop to the fullest extent possible every student's capacity to respond aesthetically to the art of music (1989, p. 153). It is interesting that Swanwick does not draw from the corpus of literature on aesthetic education in his formulation of theory. Neither does he include a single reference to Reimer's contribution to the philosophy of music education as aesthetic education over the past few decades in the United States. Whether by design or not, the author avoids using the word "aesthetic," a word that Reimer himself acknowledges to be problematic (1989, pp. xi–xiii).[3] Consequently, there is a freshness and clarity about the language for the reader who has wrestled with definitions of "aesthetic education" or "the aesthetic experience."

A second contribution Swanwick makes to music curriculum development is his reactivation and application of Basil Bernstein's (1971) concepts of knowledge classification and framing. These prove to be useful concepts for music education. For example, when applied to student assessment of the music curriculum in Britain, Swanwick points out that music in schools is so strongly classified (content determined by institution) and strongly framed (teacher-directed instruction) that school music at the secondary level seems to have a negative profile among students. It diverges from music "out there" both in idiom and in the way in which it is encountered. A similar observation was made with regard to post-elementary students in the United States in the *Manhattanville Music Curriculum Program* (see Thomas, 1970). In these cases, the institutional classification and framing of knowledge militate against readying students to participate in the pluralism of music in their environment.

If the institutional classification and framing of knowledge are to be weakened in the music curriculum, what form of assessment will be appropriate? As musical criticism is central to the author's theory of music education, so also is criticism central to assessment. When one makes a critical judgment, one declares criteria. The task is to identify those musical criteria and to define how they are assessed. Swanwick offers only very general criterion statements for the British GCSE (General Certificate of Secondary Education) examination merely to show that they are more effective and easier to generate when they are founded on an adequate theory. Of the three practical difficulties in music education addressed by Swanwick, evaluation is least explored.

It would be helpful for the reader who is not familiar with the British system of music education to have acronyms such as GCSE (General Certificate of Secondary Education) and DES (Department of Education and Science) presented in full and explained, especially since they play a prominent role in the administration, supervision, and content of music curricula in Britain. In essence, Swanwick's theory is a response to the dramatic changes that have taken place in British music education during the last decade. The following brief comparison of music education in Britain and in the United States highlights the nature of this change.

A Comparative View of Music Education in Britain and the United States

While the author makes only scant reference to music education in the United States, he does draw from the literature of music education in this country. If

---

[3] While it is beyond the scope of this review to trace the development of Swanwick's thought since he wrote this book, I will note that in a recent paper, Swanwick furthered one of his ideas (the use of "features" instead of "concepts" in music education) by comparing it to Benedetto Croce's (1953/1972) theory of intuitive or aesthetic and conceptual or intellectual knowledge. He concluded that the aesthetic is essentially "our intuitive perception of the unique in the totality of its context" (1990, pp. 11–12).

his theory can be linked with an American approach it would be that of the *Manhattanville Music Curriculum Program,* a publication cited on a few occasions in Swanwick's book. First, the use of a spiral model for a music curriculum is found in both the *MMCP* and in Swanwick's theory. However, the content of the model differs radically in both. *MMCP* employs a conceptual approach, while Swanwick focuses on the individual's engagement with music and how this is transformed with age and maturation.

Second, both sources focus on developing creativity. From the relatively dominant role assigned to composition by Swanwick and by national curriculum makers, it seems that creativity is more prominent in British music education and its development in the classroom more structured. This results in part from the national music curriculum's granting equal status to teaching listening, performing, and composing. A comparison of the U.S. and British editions of Silver Burdett and Ginn's *The World of Music* (1988) and *Silver Burdett and Ginn Music* (1989), respectively, illustrates this triangular curricular structure very clearly. The three modes of musical experience are addressed in each lesson of the British edition, thus meeting the requirements of the centralized national curriculum and determining a basic modification of the U.S. edition.

The fundamental difference between the two systems of music education lies in who classifies and frames knowledge and toward what end. In Britain, a centralized curriculum dictates the content and evaluation of criteria for music instruction. Music programs in the United States are shaped more by local needs and resources and, in recent decades, by the demands of education accountability. From Swanwick's description of the British scene, it would seem that only now the whole business of drawing up contracts and specifying criteria is surfacing in the practice of music education. He concludes: "We cannot now escape an obligation to declare our intentions and practices: whether we like it or not, the days of education 'busking' are past" (p. 154).

Will British music educators draw on American models for making instruction publicly explicit? If Swanwick's beliefs and ideas represent that group of educators, then such an occurrence is unlikely. He is critical of two features that are fundamental to American music curricula — the use of behavioral objectives and music concepts. His deep concern regarding the inappropriateness, limitations, and "undemocratic nature" of behavioral objectives for an arts subject such as music is well founded and convincingly articulated. So, too, is his identification of the danger in structuring a music curriculum around "concepts" in the music curriculum that are worthy of attention. If these compact, efficient tools for organizing a music curriculum are rejected, what are the substitutes? The author provides no clear-cut answers, but his theoretical orientation and practical speculation lead me to believe that if solutions are created, they will enrich the practice of music education at an international level.

In general terms, Swanwick identifies three "central pillars" of music education in Britain: first, a subject-centered curriculum transmitting a traditional cultural heritage or standard repertoire; second, a child-centered curriculum; and third, a curriculum that acknowledges alternative traditions to those of the first approach. Having scanned the contemporary state of British music education, the author withdraws and poses some fundamental questions about the nature of music, of musical experience, and of musical growth. Based on answers to those questions, he suggests how the diverse current theories of music education can be renewed and redesignated.

There is a logic, a coherence, and a sequence in this book that is admirable. Similar to the spiral model he uses in his theory, Swanwick returns in his own writing to ideas that he transforms with new insights. This book's originality lies in the creative synthesis of a considerable body of diverse literature, in the reactivation of theories and ideas and their fresh application to music education, and in the theoretical model constructed by Swanwick (with Tillman in its original version, 1986).

Generally, a fine balance is achieved between theory and practice. To support his arguments, Swanwick draws on results of research projects, personal observations of children making music, analysis of children's compositions, scholarly sources, and poetry. Rather than providing precise answers, his theory stimulates valuable questions. In this sense, it is a divergent theory that opens up new possibilities for future discourse. Its clear articulation lends a further positive quality for promoting discourse. The prevalence of questions may be interpreted as reflecting the contemporary transitional state of music education in Britain.

Some of the book's weak points have been identified in this review: 1) the incompatibility of Popper's philosophy of knowledge as applied to music education, in particular to the inclusion of world musics in the curriculum; 2) the inconsistency between Swanwick's focus on the common elements in introducing world musics and his criticism of the use of concepts in music education; and 3) his assumption that all readers are familiar with the British system of music education, indicated by his lack of reference notes to provide background information. The author draws on many scholarly sources and presents them in an equally scholarly manner in spite of some inconsistencies and errors.[4]

In sum, Keith Swanwick presents us with a stimulating theory of music education. Furthermore, he advances a keen perspective on the role of music in human development and its unique function in the public school curriculum. Finally, he provides a steadfast beacon to enlighten the quest for a new paradigm for the arts in education.

References

Anderson, W., & Campbell, P. S. (Eds.). (1989). *Multicultural perspectives in music education.* Reston, VA: Music Educators National Conference.

Bernstein, B. (1971). On the classification and framing of knowledge. In M. Young (Ed.), *Knowledge and control.* London: Macmillan.

[4] On p. 47, quotation from Eisner not included in "References"; p. 65, Langer quotation not dated and different format used compared with other quotation; p. 99, grammatical error, "There are instances of music which does not travel . . . "; p. 107, text omitted without ellipsis in Popper quotation.

Bruner, J. (1986). *Actual minds, possible worlds.* Cambridge, MA: Harvard University Press.

Croce, B. (1953/1972). *Aesthetic as science of expression and general linguistic.* London: Peter Owen.

Elliott, D. (1990). Music as culture: Toward a multicultural concept of arts education. *Journal of Aesthetic Education, 24*(1), 147–166.

Ellis, C. (ca. 1987). *Aboriginal education through music: Complexity within simplicity.* Unpublished paper, The University of New England, New South Wales, Australia.

Fletcher, P. (1987). *Education and music.* Oxford: Oxford University Press.

Geertz, C. (1983). *Local knowledge.* New York: Basic Books.

Green, L. (1988). *Music on deaf ears: Musical meaning, ideology, education.* New York: Manchester University Press.

Piaget, J. (1962). *Play, dreams and imitation in childhood* (C. Gattengno & F. M. Hodgson, Trans.). New York: W. W. Norton. (Original work published 1951)

Popper, K. (1972). *Objective knowledge: An evolutionary approach.* Oxford: Clarendon Press.

Reimer, B. (1989). *A philosophy of music education* (2nd ed.). Englewood Cliffs, NJ: Prentice-Hall.

Silver Burdett and Ginn Music. (1989). Morristown, NJ: Silver Burdett & Ginn.

Small, C. (1977). *Music, society, education.* London: John Calder.

Swanwick, K. (1984a). Problems of a sociological approach to pop music in schools. *British Journal of Sociology of Education, (5)*1, 49–56.

Swanwick, K. (1984b). A further note on sociology of music education. *British Journal of Sociology of Education, 5*(3), 303–307.

Swanwick, K. (1990, July). *Music curriculum development and the concept of features.* Unpublished paper presented at The Indiana Symposium on the Philosopher/Teacher in Music, the University of Indiana, Bloomington.

Swanwick, K., & Tillman, J. (1986). The sequence of musical development. *British Journal of Music Education, 3*(3), 305–309.

Thomas, R. B. (1970). *Manhattanville music curriculum program: Synthesis.* Bardonia, NY: Media Materials.

Vulliamy, G., & Shepherd, J. (1984). Sociology and music education: A response to Swanwick. *British Journal of Sociology of Education, 5*(1), 57–76.

Vulliamy, G., & Shepherd, J. (1985). Sociology and music education: A further response to Swanwick. *British Journal of Sociology of Education, 6*(2), 225–229.

Walker, R. (1990). *Musical beliefs: Psychological, mythical, and educational perspectives.* New York: Teachers College Press.

The world of music. (1988). Morristown, NJ: Silver Burdett & Ginn.

Book Notes

MERRYL RUTH GOLDBERG

The following reviews appeared in the Harvard Educational Review *between 1989 and 1991. These books have been selected because of their relevance to the arts and education.*

ARTISTIC INTELLIGENCES: IMPLICATIONS FOR EDUCATION
edited by William J. Moody.
New York: Teachers College Press, 1990. 195 pp. $20.95.

"The Year of the Arts," a year-long initiative at the University of South Carolina, culminated in the Artistic Intelligences Conference in April 1989. The conference's purpose was to consider the implications of Howard Gardner's theory of multiple intelligences and its relation to arts education. The contributors to *Artistic Intelligences,* which is a collection of the papers presented at the conference, hope that it "will serve as a resource and catalyst for those who believe in educating the several intelligences and are willing to work for educational reform" (pp. ix–x).

Writing from his perspective as a musician, Moody describes his concept of the book's organization as a modified sonata-allegro form with "artistic intelligences" as the leitmotif. "Part I presents thematic material, Part II is the development section, Part III describes contrapuntal techniques, and Part IV is the recapitulation" (p. xi). The thematic section, Part I, includes Harold Taylor's "The Arts in a Democracy," which is followed by an essay in which Howard Gardner describes his theory of multiple intelligences. Part II, the development section, includes articles by Eliot Eisner, Mary Hatwood Futrell, Harriet Keyserling, Charlie G. Williams, Rose Maree Myers, and Warren Bennett Newman. Newman's article examines the effect of standardized testing in relation to the arts, and is followed by responses from Gardner and Eisner. Part III, contrapuntal techniques, includes articles on artistic intelligences and their relation to general education, visual arts, creative writing, dance, movement, acting, and music, written by Charles Hoffer, Charles Elliot, and Peter Werner. The recapitulation, Part IV, begins with an article by Maxine Greene, "Arts Education in the Humanities: Toward a Breaking of the Boundaries," followed by an article by Charles Fowler, and, finally, a summary and "coda" by Moody.

When asked if "talents" weren't really the subject of his theory of intelligences, Gardner, who spoke at the conference, responded that "nomenclature was not something he would quibble about if natural ability in linguistics and in mathematics were also called talents" (p. ix). "The roses that smell sweet in our culture are labeled 'intelligences,'" continues Moody, "and Gardner's theory identifies at least seven, including those practiced by the 'talented'" (p. ix).

The book includes a chapter by Gardner that raises interesting, provocative questions. Though written in an inviting tone with a fluid style, it is also authoritative. For example, Gardner defines intelligence as "an ability to solve problems or to fashion a product, to make something that is valued in at least one culture" (p. 16). He describes creativity as parallel to his definition of intelligence, and states that "the important point is that a person is creative in a domain" (p. 21). He defines creativity as "the ability to solve problems or to make something or to pose questions regularly in a domain; those questions are initially novel but are eventually accepted in one or more cultures" (p. 21). The similarity of these two definitions is at once exhilarating and distressing. While it is exhilarating to think of intelligence as creativity, the reader is left wondering how Gardner truly separates the two. Is creativity a part of intelligence, or are they separate, as "parallel" would suggest? The question of the relationship of intelligence to creativity remains ambiguous and relatively unexplored.

In another realm, Gardner builds his case by refuting many claims that he assigns to Piaget. For instance, he asserts that "Piaget thought he was studying all of intelligence, but it is my claim that he was really studying logical-mathematical intelligence" (p. 19). While many people may believe that Piaget concentrated on logico-mathematical intelligence, this interpretation is inconsistent with the thoughts and language Piaget used in many of his writings. In his early books he discussed extensively "sensory motor intelligence," as in *Play Dreams and Imitation* and *The Origins of Intelligence;* in the *Child's Conception of Geometry, The Child's Conception of Space,* and *The Child's Conception of Number,* Piaget discusses "spatial knowing" at length. Could these Piagetian concepts be translated as the forerunners of Gardner's kinesthetic and spatial intelligences? The authoritative and exclusive claims Gardner makes may deceive a reader unfamiliar with Piagetian theory.

In writing about Piagetian stages, Gardner states that "some people pass through them much more quickly, and those people would be bright people" (p. 4). However, Piaget — during his 1964 visits to the University of California at Berkeley and Cornell University, and in the 1977 film *Piaget on Piaget* (Yale University) — talks at length about how the environment might affect the rate at which people pass through stages of development. He makes the point that all people pass through the stages, not that an individual is more or less intelligent as a result of the rate at which she or he passes through the stages.

Finally, in its definitions of intelligence and creativity, Gardner's view of culture is somewhat limited. Most of his examples of people who fit his categories of intelligences are from Western cultures, or, as in the case of Gandhi, have been educated in the Western culture. Thus, what Gardner actually means by culture seems limited, at best. Moreover, how non-Western cultures figure into his theory is not clear to the reader.

As is evident from the critique and questions raised in the book, Gardner's theory of multiple intelligences stimulates lively debate among theorists, educators, and artists, which is in keeping with his intent that his theory will "contribute to more effective educational practice."[1] This current volume is a testimony to this phenomenon. Eliot Eisner puts it this way:

> It is . . . apparent that the idea of multiple intelligence is more a vision of educational possibility than it is an empirical fact. One of the things that has attracted so many people to the notion is the promise that it holds, its social and educational potential, beyond whether the facts of the case can support the idea. I believe that eventually the facts will support the idea, but what is really attractive to me is that the concept has something to do with the way we run our lives, the way we run our schools, and how we regard human capacities. (p. 31)

Artistic Intelligences: Implications for Education could very well be the "catalyst" that Moody hopes will spark the debate around educational reform and frame the vision that Eisner writes about. Taken as a whole, it is a unique collection of impressive ideas from educators and theorists in the "domain" of the arts that has the potential to influence — and even revolutionize — educational thought and policy.

GROWING UP COMPLETE: THE IMPERATIVE FOR MUSIC EDUCATION; THE REPORT OF THE NATIONAL COMMISSION ON MUSIC EDUCATION by the Music Educators National Conference.
Reston, VA: Music Educators National Conference, March 1991. 46 pp. $7.95.

It is clear from recent education policy decisions that most educational policy-makers do not consider the arts as basic education. Nationwide cuts in education budgets have resulted in more and more arts programs being eliminated or replaced with one-time performances by artists in the schools.

Growing Up Complete addresses several concerns relative to the omission of music and other arts in children's basic education, including why the arts are critical in shaping children's aesthetic, cognitive, and emotional development. The document also offers policy recommendations for administrators, educators, and parents on how to make music a basic component in the education of all children.

The report begins with a declaration of concern that, while educational reform in the 1980s made front-page news in light of low test scores in math and science, any discussion of the importance of the arts remained silent:

---

[1] Howard Gardner, *Frames of Mind* (New York: Basic Books, 1983), p. xiv.

> We believe such nearsighted concern shortchanges our children because
> it leaves them only half-educated. Since the beginnings of civilization,
> music has been crucial to quality education. (p. vii)

To that end, members of the National Commission on Music Education call
for all who care about education to "destroy, once and for all, the myth that
education in music and the other arts is mere 'curricular icing'" (p. vii). They
continue:

> We call on all who love the arts to insist that instruction in music and
> other arts be reestablished as basic to education, not only by virtue of
> their intrinsic worth, but because they are fundamental to what it means
> to be an educated person. (p. vii)

The wording of the declaration, which calls for a "reestablishment" of arts in
the schools, is particularly telling: Although arts advocates have been through
this battle before, the victory has never been secure or uncontested. Thus, the
editors of *Growing Up Complete* suggest that now is perhaps the time to work
toward a lasting and peaceful negotiation that includes all subjects. When it
comes to "basic education," the arts provide a connection to fundamental concerns of culture, civilization, and history, as well as a way of expressing such
knowing; they also provide basic spatial, kinesthetic, and aesthetic skills. "Education cannot get more basic than that," conclude the editors of this report.

Following the declaration of concern, the report outlines the imperative for
music education in four chapters. In chapter four, "Making It Happen: Mount-
ing a National Effort," the editors identify several ways to approach engendering
change. The report concludes with artists' testimonies and a list of organizations
that endorse and support the arts and education.

What arts advocates might find particularly helpful in this book are the ratio-
nales for the arts as a basic aspect of education, which include quotes of artists,
philosophers, and educators from Plato to Wynton Marsalis. In chapter three,
for example, Howard Gardner's theory of multiple intelligences, musical intelligence in particular, is touched on as a source of relatively new theoretical and
academic underpinnings that provides a rationale for the responsibility of
schools to include the arts in education.

Arguments are presented in support of the arts — both for their own sake
and as an aid to the learning of other subjects such as reading, spelling, and
mathematics, and also for the development of listening, and motor and verbal
abilities. The editors also consider the qualities and skills children garner from
performing.

As a report and guide for a call to action, *Growing Up Complete* fulfills the goals
of its sponsors. Readers, and particularly arts advocates, will undoubtedly find
this document useful and full of quotable sound-bites. Although this report gives
somewhat superficial coverage of a vast subject, the footnotes and citations at
the end of each chapter provide the interested reader with ample resources to
examine the subject in greater detail.

This report serves an important purpose as it unites many voices that advocate for the use of music and arts education and the arts as a way to allow all children to "grow up complete."

FREE PLAY: IMPROVISATION IN LIFE AND ART
by Stephen Nachmanovitch.
Los Angeles: Jeremy P. Tarcher, 1990. 208 pp. $16.95.

"Paint as you like and die happy" (Henry Miller) are the first words in Stephen Nachmanovitch's *Free Play: Improvisation in Life and Art* — a terrific opening for a discussion of creativity, life, and learning. From those first words, Nachmanovitch, a musician and writer influenced greatly by the late Gregory Bateson, takes the reader on a journey that explores the inner sources of unhindered play and creative energy.

Nachmanovitch writes about our inner sources of spontaneous creation. The natural question that arises is: "What is the source we tap when we create?" (p. 5). For Nachmanovitch, one source is improvisation. "When I first found myself improvising, I felt with great excitement that I was onto something, a kind of spiritual connectedness that went far beyond the scope of music making. . . . Looking into the moment of improvisation, I was uncovering patterns related to every kind of creativity. . . . I came to see improvisation as the master key to creativity" (p. 6).

For Nachmanovitch, "the heart of improvisation is the free play of consciousness as it draws, writes, paints, and plays the raw material emerging from the unconscious. Such play entails a certain degree of risk" (p. 9). Play is a part of us all. According to Jean Piaget, imitation and play form a major role in the child's development. But how often do adults play? Perhaps, as Nachmanovitch suggests, adults might have much to learn from regaining or recapturing a sense of play in their everyday lives. The question follows: How could play develop and release creative powers? Nachmanovitch addresses this by equating improvisation in the arts with play, and he does so with remarkable fluidity. He provides the reader with examples of musicians at "play" — improvising. He contrasts, for instance, a jazz musician improvising a solo with what many of us will recognize as more common: a skilled performer relying on the written notes. "Many musicians are fabulously skilled at playing the black dots on the printed page, but mystified by how the dots got there. . . . Music theory does not help here; it teaches rules of grammar, but not what to say" (p. 9). Isn't this true of much of modern-day learning? Children learn fabulous skills, yet are unable to make them their own.

Nachmanovitch has the keen ability to bring his experiences clearly to the reader in order to provoke reflection. His writing style, often metaphoric, provides "food for thought" with a special spice. For example, his opening line in the chapter "Playing Together" begins, "The beauty of playing together is meeting in the One." He continues, "It is astonishing how often it happens that two

musicians meet for the first time, coming perhaps from very different backgrounds and traditions, and before they have exchanged two words they begin
improvising music together that demonstrates wholeness, structure, and clear
communication" (p. 94). Following this, it is easy to imagine two children meeting on the playground, perhaps from differing backgrounds, and before they
have exchanged two words they are running and spinning about, inventing paths
and games around the swings and trees. This is the essence of improvisation —
play, a kind of freedom that allows spontaneous creative energy. Though often
recognized in the child, Nachmanovitch leads us toward recognizing it in ourselves.

Free Play includes a bibliography, several illustrations, and absolutely wonderful quotations from such free players as Stephane Grappelli, William Blake, W.
B. Yeats, Carl Jung, Vincent van Gogh, Gregory Bateson, and Martha Graham.
This book is important not only because it delves into the creative process, but
also because Nachmanovitch creates the opportunity for the reader to get in
touch with her/his own creative possibilities and abilities. He helps the reader
think about and make use of her/his own natural playfulness as a resource of
creativity. As such, this is an essential book for everyone — teachers, parents,
administrators, and researchers.

THE ARTS AT BLACK MOUNTAIN COLLEGE
by Mary Emma Harris.
Cambridge, MA: MIT Press, 1987. 315 pp. $29.95.

At Black Mountain College, education was to be a preparation for life. Belief in
democracy was an unquestionable assumption underlying the college's structure
and philosophy. Central to the college's program was the role of the arts in the
curriculum. "At Black Mountain the arts were to be given a position equal to
that of other subjects; and for the beginning student, they were to be the most
important courses in the curriculum" writes Mary Emma Harris. "This was a
critical aspect of the college's holistic approach to education, through which the
student was to learn not just information but a method of dealing with that
information as well as values and emotional maturity" (p. 7).

Harris's largely historical account of the college is detailed, well written, and
lively. Original voices, documents, pictures, musical scores, and works of art are
interwoven throughout the text. Black Mountain College, located in North Carolina, lasted only twenty-four years, from 1933 to 1957, and was continually beset
by financial woes. The extraordinary legacy of Black Mountain College includes
the work and thought of an abundance of creative people such as Willem de
Kooning, Agnes de Mille, John Cage, Paul Taylor, Robert Rauschenberg, Arthur
Penn, John Dewey, Walter Gropius, Dorothea Rockburne, Carl Jung, Max Ler-
ner, Franz Kline, and Albert Einstein. Harris's account of this center of experi-
mentalism serves a unique purpose today, not only as a work of educational

history, but as a catalyst for those who think about educational reform. Harris writes that she does not "look with nostalgia" or hope for the creation of a new Black Mountain in writing this book. She does hope in the preface "that the story of Black Mountain will bring the reader to a richer understanding of his or her own cultural heritage and the relevance of the college's ideas to the present time."

Education that denies culture denies life. Educational reform without the inclusion of the arts is not reform at all. Black Mountain College idealists valued life, culture, the arts, and reform. Though deemed "radical" by some, one cannot help but think that this tiny college was not radical at all, but humane in an otherwise insane world. As Harris writes in the preface, "Black Mountain College was conceived at a critical moment in American and international history." The "college's founding occurred simultaneously with the appointment of Adolf Hitler as chancellor of Germany in January 1933, with the closing of the Bauhaus by the Nazis, and the beginning of the persecution of artists, intellectuals, and Jews on the European continent." It was in the spirit of reform and idealism that Black Mountain College was born and from which it was to emerge as a model of education and humanity.

"Participation in community life was an integral part of the student's educational experience" (p. 7). Faculty members, their families, and students all lived on campus and ate in the communal dining hall. The school was coeducational, which, as John Andrew Rice, a founder of the college, said, was to mean "here [women and men] should learn to know that their relationship to each other, both while they are in college and afterwards, is to be, in the main, not one of opposites, but of those who live upon the common ground of humanity" (p. 7). Issues that involved the entire community were resolved at student and community meetings.

Harris's account of Black Mountain includes a faculty and student roster, along with an extensive listing of archival, library, and private collections of the college's history. As a historical piece, this book captures the depth and spirit of a tremendous group of diverse artists, thinkers, educators, and idealists as they practiced their beliefs and dreams in their educational community. It provides a resource for educators who are dedicated to culture and the arts as an unquestionable basis of education. The book can also stand on its own as an "art" book, filled with photographs, poetry, monographs, and musical scores of many of the college's now famous artists and creators. Reading this book will surely lend insight to those who continually question the role of education and life; for those who find themselves striving and searching for something better; for those willing to test idealism with practice; and for those who understand that reform must continue always. As Harris states in the preface: "This book is presented as a beginning, both for the reader and the author, who anticipate that new materials, new information, and new ideas will emerge from the conversation generated by its publication."

MULTICULTURAL PERSPECTIVES IN MUSIC EDUCATION
edited by William M. Anderson and Patricia Shehan Campbell.
Reston, VA: Music Educators National Conference, 1989. 326 pp. $39.50.

This book begins, "The content of music programs in American schools has historically been associated with the art and traditional musics of western Europe" (p. viii). In the 1970s, the Music Educators National Conference (MENC) recognized that Western art and Western music don't speak to the ever-changing, multicultural classrooms throughout the United States. MENC then established a Minority Concerns Commission and a Multicultural Awareness Commission "with the intention of raising the level of consciousness and promoting the use of traditional musics of many cultures in the curriculum" (p. ix).

The principal aim of this book is to provide a pragmatic approach to the integration of world music traditions in general music classes from upper elementary through high school. That aim parallels MENC's philosophy of "'Music for *every* child — every child *for* music.' Embedded in this slogan is the knowledge that school music must be more broadly defined to encompass the ethnic diversity of American schools and society" (p. viii).

The book begins with an introduction and rationale, followed by chapters on various world musics. Each chapter begins with an introduction to the region and a map, followed by lesson plans that include singing, listening, playing, and sometimes dancing. Because each chapter is authored by a different contributor, each has its own flavor.

Although this book is not comprehensive and certainly not exhaustive of world music (how could it be?), it is a valiant attempt: MENC begins to bridge the gap between multicultural education and music education. The bibliographies, discographies, and filmographies (again not comprehensive or exhaustive) provide resources for teachers as they begin thinking about how to incorporate the different musics of the world into their classrooms.

One drawback of this book is its recipe-style format. Teachers are given lesson plans in each chapter. These lesson plans might prove useful, but only if teachers view them as possibilities or outlines to improvise from, not prescriptions. Teachers should also be urged to tap into their communities for resources, since communities themselves offer multiple traditions and ways of understanding.

Multicultural education is aimed at recognizing and validating differences. *Multicultural Perspectives in Music Education* begins to bring music education into this wonderfully rich mode of educating, understanding, and living.

ART IN A DEMOCRACY
edited by Doug Blandy and Kristin G. Congdon.
New York: Teachers College Press, 1987. 201 pp. $27.95, $16.95 (paper).

A new and provocative book for educators of all disciplines, *Art in a Democracy* provides a forum for thought and reflection on questions regarding the role of art in a democratic society. The book is a collection of essays divided into five sections: Individual Differences, Cultural Pluralism, and Social Role of Valorization; Public Dialogue on Art; The Citizens' Responsibility to Individual and Group Processes; Freedom of Aesthetic Choice in Work and Play; and Response to *Art in a Democracy*.

The chapters explore questions such as: How do ideal democratic values affect the selection of art? What are the motivations for producing art? What are the implications of these factors in culturally complex societies trying to achieve political democracy? Are criticism and dialogue in the arts based on hierarchical or democratic values? Do they support and encourage freedom of choice?

The editors address "freedom of expression, empowering those who have been left out of 'the system,' [the] social role of valorization, cultural pluralism, feminism, multiple levels of intelligence, the recognition and acceptance and expansion of different organizational structures" (p. xv). Contributing authors debate questions of multiculturalism, art, and multicultural democracy.

The editors and contributing authors continually carry the conversation from theory into practice, stating in the introduction, "The reader will note the strong desire to recognize the artistic process and aesthetic response as integral to our lives, not only preserved in museums but to be practiced in our day-to-day experiences in the educational process."

Recommended for all educators, *Art in a Democracy* will be particularly helpful in broadening understanding of the importance of art to education in any political society. In addition to the editors, contributors to this volume include Barbara Ann Boyer, F. Graeme Chalmers, Georgia C. Collins, Karen Hamblen, Vincent Lanier, June King McFee, Russ McKnight, and Mary Ann Stankiewicz.

WOMEN COMPOSERS: THE LOST TRADITION FOUND
by Diane Peacock Jezic.
New York: The Feminist Press, 1988. 222 pp. $12.95 (paper).

Diane Peacock Jezic guides the reader through the lives and works of twenty-five Western women composers from the eleventh century to the present. Her comprehensive, readable approach to this project engages the reader immediately. Each of the twenty-five chapters is devoted to a composer, her life and work, an analysis of one to four compositions, a selected list of her compositions, and a selected bibliography and discography for further reference. In the case of living composers, the reader is provided with information on how to contact the composers themselves.

Jezic states that she selected the composers and musical examples with three goals in mind: 1) to represent the major periods and genres of music history; 2) to represent the best of what women have composed in those genres typically associated with them, namely songs, piano pieces, and small chamber music works, usually featuring stringed instruments, flute, and/or piano; and 3) to present some nonstereotypical genres, especially instrumental music, or excerpts from the genres usually associated with men (opera, cantata, the nonet), to dispel the myth that women can't compose in these areas. A balance was also sought between vocal and instrumental music.

Especially noteworthy and informative is the extensive supplementary information provided by Jezic in the appendices, which include the names and addresses of record companies that feature works by women; a chart of styles and genres of over fifty women composers, along with the more familiar male composers, from 850 through the 1940s; additional composers born after 1920 and their favored genres; and a selected listing of women conductors.

Recordings of thirty-eight compositions produced by Marnie Hall in conjunction with the book are available on two cassettes from Leonarda Productions. The recordings follow the chronology of the book. For cassette recordings or a complete catalog, write to Leonarda Productions, P.O. Box 1736, Cathedral Station, New York, NY, 10025, or call (212) 666-7697.

Women Composers: The Lost Tradition Found is an essential addition to music, arts, and humanities libraries and courses. If one question could be asked of Ms. Jezic, it would be, "When can we expect more?"

NO MAN'S LAND: THE PLACE OF THE WOMAN WRITER IN THE
TWENTIETH CENTURY, VOLUME I: THE WAR OF THE WORDS
by Sandra M. Gilbert and Susan Gubar.
New Haven: Yale University Press, 1989. 320 pp. $25.00, $11.95 (paper).

NO MAN'S LAND: THE PLACE OF THE WOMAN WRITER IN THE
TWENTIETH CENTURY, VOLUME II: SEXCHANGES
by Sandra M. Gilbert and Susan Gubar.
New Haven: Yale University Press, 1989. 455 pp. $29.95.

Volumes I and II of *No Man's Land* are part of a three-volume work that brings feminist theory to bear on modern English and American literature. Focusing on both male and female writers, Gilbert and Gubar survey social, literary, and linguistic conflicts between the sexes as revealed in texts by nineteenth- and twentieth-century writers from Tennyson to Woolf, from Hemingway to Plath. Joyce Carol Oates said of Volume I: "Fast, funny, profound in its theoretical assertions, and deliciously irreverent in its asides. Male readers and critics will ignore it at their own peril."

Volume II, *Sexchanges*, expands on the authors' claim that the sexual battles they explored in *The War of the Words* were "inevitably associated with radical 'sexchanges,' as well as with notably sexualized visions of change and exchange" (p. xi) in the work lives of both women and men. Specifically, the authors argue that the "sexes battle because sex roles change, but, when the sexes battle, sex itself (that is, eroticism) changes" (p. xi).

The authors hope that, taken together, the volumes will help illuminate the "radical transformations of culture" that we all face: transformations in literature, marriage and the family, education and the professions, in which "scattered armies of men and women all too often clash by day and by night" (p. xiii). Ultimately, the authors seek to describe and not prescribe, for their goal is to record and analyze the history that has "made us who we are" through the lens of literature.

Provocative and witty, these two volumes inspire reflection. They bring us all, women and men, face to face with the powerful domain of literature, culture, and life as it has been represented in words throughout the twentieth century. Only one question: When will Volume III be ready?

THEATRE IN SEARCH OF SOCIAL CHANGE: THE RELATIVE SIGNIFICANCE
OF DIFFERENT THEATRICAL APPROACHES
by Kees P. Epskamp. CESO Paperback No. 7.
The Hague: Center for the Study of Education in Developing Countries, 1989.
209 pp. $12.50 (paper).

Theatre in Search of Social Change explores the role of theater in education by examining many world cultures. The central question raised by Kees Epskamp is how the sociology of theater balances with the developmental processes of learning:

> What is the educative role of theater in processes of social change and development and how is the use of theater as a small-scale medium to be evaluated in realizing development projects based on a participatory or interventionist model? (p. 11)

Epskamp describes several types of theater, including "folk," "court," and "popular." He explores the historical antecedents of "Theater for Development," as well as "Popular Theater from an Educative Point of View" and the "Performing Arts as Instruments of Intervention." Epskamp's perspectives on theater for development emerge from critical pedagogy and are "strongly influenced by the ideas of Paulo Freire, as derived from his *Pedagogy of the Oppressed,* in which an open dialogue is an important emancipatory development instrument" (p. 12). Thus, he discusses the role of theater for development, and asks if theater is an instrument that can be used against oppression. Epskamp skillfully addresses issues of class, age, and gender in the many cultures visited, including Java, Bali, Mexico, Botswana, Nigeria, Tanzania, Jamaica, Bangladesh, Cuba, and the Philippines. The thematic importance of culture is evident throughout this volume. The book provides insight into the use of the arts as critical pedagogy and an instrument for social change. It also contains a lengthy multilingual bibliography of related articles.

MUSEUMS AND UNIVERSITIES: NEW PATHS FOR CONTINUING EDUCATION
edited by Janet W. Solinger. American Council on Education/Macmillan
Series in Higher Education.
New York: Macmillan, 1990. 351 pp. $29.95.

Today, museums are places where cultures and societies are preserved, often in
glass cases or hung from walls or ceilings. Visitors tour through history or cultures at a distance, looking and perhaps reading, stopping for brief forays into
a world either different from their own or strikingly the same. The collections
are a testimony to cultural heritages, mostly past. Yet, as Janet Solinger writes,
"when the ancient Greeks referred to a museum (Gk. *Mouseion*) the word primarily defined a center of learning. Thus, although a Greek museum might well
have contained statues or other objects dedicated to the muses and their arts, it
was the educational and intellectual aspects of the site that made it a museum .
. ." (p. 1). It is precisely that connection, the museum as a center of learning,
that is the basis of this edited collection.

Though long recognized as resources for schoolchildren, museums have been
traditionally attended by adults as a leisure-time activity. Recent interest and
growth in adult education programs has, however, greatly expanded museums'
contribution to lifelong learning. *Museums and Universities* explores the museum-
education dialectic through thirteen diverse essays written by professors, cura-
tors, and administrators (of both museums and universities). The essays touch
upon current trends in adult and museum education, meeting the learning expectations of adults, formal and informal education, community participation,
college and museum partnerships, and the evaluation of such programs.

THE CHALLENGE TO REFORM ARTS EDUCATION: WHAT ROLE CAN
RESEARCH PLAY?
edited by David B. Pankratz and Kevin V. Mulcahy.
New York: ACA Books, 1989. 98 pp. $9.95 (paper).

This book assesses the changing climate of the arts in educational reform and
research. Various authors examine the increasingly complex environment in
which it is essential for new school reform policies to encompass the arts. Questions raised in this collection include: What role can research play in arts education? What research do we have? What research do we need? Can research
improve practice and policy development? In his contribution, "The Need for
Policy Studies in Arts Education," Samuel Hope of the National Office for the
Arts Accreditation in Higher Education argues that policy research studies are
essential if the quality of debate within the field is to be lively and provocative.

Issues critical to research in arts education, the need for policy studies, and
implications of moving research theory into practice are raised by Margaret
DiBlasio of the University of Minnesota, Jerrold Ross of New York University,
Brent Wilson of Penn State University, and Theodore Zernich of the University
of Illinois. In the last contribution to this volume, Kevin Mulcahy addresses

"Toward Civilization through the Arts," which provides a postscript to the National Endowment for the Arts report, *Toward Civilization: A Report on Arts Education.* This collection will be of interest to policymakers both in and out of the arts and to all educators interested in reform.

ALL EARS: HOW TO CHOOSE AND USE RECORDED MUSIC FOR CHILDREN
by Jill Jarnow.
New York: Penguin Books, 1991. 210 pp. $17.95, $9.95 (paper).

All Ears is a guide and resource listing of recorded children's music for parents and early childhood educators. In this book, Jill Jarnow describes many recordings in depth. She also provides information about where these recordings can be purchased, as well as how to use them effectively. Indexed by subject and age-appropriateness, *All Ears* includes more than two hundred recordings by musicians such as Pete Seeger, the Weavers, Ella Jenkins, Sharon, Louis and Bram, ROSENSHONTZ, and Raffi. Jarnow also discusses the importance of music in the daily lives and development of children from infancy through young adulthood, paying particular attention to the role of parents in listening to recorded music with their children.

The book is a helpful, thorough review of music and recordings for children in terms of American folk traditions; however, it does not address world musical traditions and cultures, or the vast cultural diversity within the United States. Nonetheless, this collection can be useful to educators and parents who are interested in learning about the educational potential of recorded music in their children's lives.

LATIN AMERICAN ART: AN INTRODUCTION TO WORKS OF THE 20TH CENTURY
by Dorothy Chaplik, foreword by Angel Hurtado.
Jefferson, NC: McFarland, 1989. 207 pp. $29.95.

This is an indispensable reference book for art educators and students, scholars of Latin America, historians, and those who are dedicated to broadening their own and their students' understanding of art in a world sense. Dorothy Chaplik has consulted a most impressive number of books, catalogues, and articles in preparation for this volume. As Angel Hurtado writes in the foreword, "I confess I had no idea the material was so extensive. . . . I am convinced that her study will serve to stimulate still greater interest in an area of Latin American art which up until now has been unduly neglected" (p. 4).

The book includes biographical information on each of the artists studied; critical analyses of several paintings; reproductions of paintings, including a color section; a glossary; and an extensive bibliography that not only addresses references to Latin art, but also includes references to each artist reviewed in the collection. This book — which provides a detailed and in-depth discussion about a subject that has not been, yet needs to be, recognized or widely studied — is an important contribution to art, education, and history.

THE GLOBAL ANTHOLOGY OF JEWISH WOMEN WRITERS
edited by Robert Kalechofsky and Roberta Kalechofsky.
Marblehead, MA: Micah Publications, 1990. 448 pp. $14.95.

This anthology traces the writings of Jewish women from the enlightenment era to the present. Thirty-four Jewish women writers from Europe, the Soviet Union, Israel, Arabic countries, Latin America, South Africa, and the United States are represented. It includes the writings of Emma Goldman on birth control and women in the Spanish Civil War, Eugenia Ginzburg on the imprisonment of women in the Gulag, Barbara Mujica on class conflict and revolutionary tension in a South American country, poetry by Nelly Sachs, and reflections of Hannah Arendt.

The volume is divided into five sections: Emerging; I Take the Shape on the Loom of History; And on Waves of Revolution; With Poetry and Reflections; and, finally, On Love, Sex, and Marriage in the Sixth Millennium. This book is an exciting addition to the Echad series of anthologies of Jewish writing from around the world, whose previous titles include: *Latin American Jewish Writings, South African Jewish Voices,* and *Jewish Writing from Down Under: Australia and New Zealand.* This book would appeal to those interested in women's literature, women's issues, feminism, and history.

A HISTORY OF ART EDUCATION: INTELLECTUAL AND SOCIAL CURRENTS
IN TEACHING THE VISUAL ARTS
by Arthur D. Elfand.
New York: Teachers College Press, 1990. 320 pp. $43.95, $22.95 (paper).

This volume is the first new history of art education to be published in thirty-five years. It is a book about the teaching of the visual arts throughout the history of education. Elfand not only describes events throughout the history of art in education, but also examines the institutional settings of art education, the social forces that have shaped art education, and the impact of various trends that have influenced present practice. In addition, Elfand places art history in relation to the developments in general education. He places particular emphasis on the nineteenth and twentieth centuries, though he delves as far back as the Middle Ages. Elfand believes that "a sense of elitism clings to the teaching of the visual arts. Many schools regard the arts as special subjects to be pursued by a privileged or talented few" (p. 1). To see how these attitudes arose, he takes the reader back to the beginnings of education in Western culture.

This book will be useful as a text in history of art education courses, as a supplement to general history courses, and as a resource to students, professors, and researchers.

BLACK MOUNTAIN COLLEGE: SPROUTED SEEDS, AN ANTHOLOGY OF
PERSONAL ACCOUNTS
edited by Mervin Lane.
Knoxville: University of Tennessee Press, 1990. 346 pp. $32.50.

Black Mountain College, an experimental and revolutionary school that operated in North Carolina from 1933 to 1957, is remembered for its importance to education and art. Its students and teachers included such well-known figures as Josef Albers, Merce Cummingham, John Cage, William de Kooning, Agnes de Mille, and Franz Kline. *Black Mountain College* follows three other outstanding personal accounts of the college: Fielding Dawson's *The Black Mountain Book* (1970), Martin Duberman's *Black Mountain: An Exploration in Community* (1972), and Mary Emma Harris's *The Arts at Black Mountain College* (1987; see pp. 142–143).

In his latest book, the personal accounts and reminiscences are arranged chronologically according to the writers' years of attendance at the school. The book includes ninety essays, poems, plays, and reproductions of artwork by former students. This volume will be of particular interest to those who are curious about the philosophy, experiments, and daily life of the Black Mountain College community. Educators and others who are interested in the arts, learning, and creativity will also find it enjoyable and informative reading.

ART, MIND AND EDUCATION: RESEARCH FROM PROJECT ZERO
edited by Howard Gardner and David Perkins.
Urbana: University of Illinois Press, 1989. 170 pp. $19.95, $8.95 (paper).

This book is an eclectic mixture of articles written by various members and friends of Project Zero, an interdisciplinary research project founded in 1967 at Harvard University by Nelson Goodman. Drawing upon the disciplines of philosophy, developmental and cognitive psychology, neurology, education, the arts, and the sciences, members of Project Zero have researched symbolic development, while focusing on cognitive abilities. This volume includes articles on children's drawings, fiction for children, children and nonliteral language, musical perceptual knowledge, musical development with computers, arts education in the People's Republic of China, musical expression, metaphor, and art as understanding.

PLAYDANCING
by Diane Lynch Fraser.
Pennington, NJ: Princeton Book Company, 1991. 122 pp. $19.95, $12.95 (paper).

By the same author as *DancePlay: Creative Movement for Young Children, Playdancing* is written for the early childhood teacher. The author's premise is that the "movement, or 'dancing,' of young children has great meaning and value in their lives. It cannot and should not be ignored or trivialized" (p. ix). Fraser believes that there is a "natural link between the young child's spontaneous movement expression, and her ability to communicate and problem solve creatively" (p. ix). *Playdancing* includes activities and ideas that are designed to reinforce the "magical connection" between movement and creativity. Written primarily for classroom teachers with little or no dance experience, this book is useful for creative arts teachers and parents as well.

DIMENSIONS OF MUSICAL THINKING
edited by Eunice Boardman.
Reston, VA: Music Educators National Conference, 1989. 120 pp. $10.00 (paper).

This collection is concerned with the relation of thinking to the study of music. Articles address musical thinking in the following areas: the general music classroom, choral and instrumental rehearsals, special education classrooms, and teacher education classrooms. Articles include "Metacognition: A Dimension of Musical Thinking" by Lenore Pogonowski, "Critical and Creative Musical Thinking" by Mark DeTurk, "Musical Thinking Processes" and "Musical Thinking and Technology" by Brian Moore, "Musical Thinking and the Young Child" by Barbara Alvarez, and "Core Thinking Skills in Music" by Janet Barrett.

TEACHING MUSIC IN THE SECONDARY SCHOOLS (4TH ED.)
by Charles R. Hoffer.
Belmont, CA: Wadsworth Publishing, 1991. 399 pp. $40.50.

Teaching Music in the Secondary Schools is a comprehensive resource for students of music education and secondary teachers who are interested in learning more about the subject. The book begins with a philosophical rationale for teaching music in the schools: what should be taught, how it should be taught, and to whom. Throughout the book, Hoffer balances theory, practice, and philosophy as he examines many issues related to the teaching of music, including psychology, ethics, aesthetics, musical expression, performance, computers, discipline, assessment, and the transfer of music to other subjects. Each chapter concludes with a list of references, recommended readings, related questions, and suggested project ideas.

Resource Guide

The following publications and recordings have been recommended by the editors and contributing authors.

CONTRIBUTING AUTHORS' CHOICES

Aesthetic Education

recommended by Maxine Greene, author of "Texts and Margins"

Arnheim, Rudolf. *Visual Thinking.* Berkeley: University of California Press, 1969.

Berger, John. *Ways of Seeing.* New York: Penguin Books, 1972.

Brook, Peter. *The Empty Space.* New York: Atheneum, 1968.

Cohen, Selma Jeanne (Ed.). *The Modern Dance: Seven Statements of Belief.* Middletown, CT: Wesleyan University Press, 1973.

Danto, Arthur. *The Transfiguration of the Commonplace: A Philosophy of Art.* Cambridge, MA: Harvard University Press, 1981.

Dewey, John. *Art as Experience.* New York: Capricorn Books, 1959.

Dufrenne, Mikel. *The Phenomenology of Aesthetic Experience.* Evanston, IL: Northwestern University Press, 1973.

Gombrich, Ernst. *Art and Illusion: A Study in the Psychology of Pictorial Representation.* Princeton, NJ: Princeton University Press, 1969.

Goodman, Nelson. *Languages of Art: An Approach to a Theory of Symbols.* Indianapolis: Hackett, 1976.

Isenberg, Arnold. *Aesthetics and the Theory of Criticism.* Chicago: University of Chicago Press, 1973.

Iser, Wolfgang. *The Act of Reading: A Theory of Aesthetic Response.* Baltimore: Johns Hopkins University Press, 1978.

Langer, Susanne. *Problems of Art.* New York: Scribner, 1957.

Marcuse, Herbert. *The Aesthetic Dimension: Toward a Critique of Marxist Aesthetic.* Boston: Beacon Press, 1978.

Osborne, Harold. *Aesthetics and Art Theory: A Historical Introduction.* New York: E. P. Dutton, 1970.

Rosenblatt, Louise M. *The Reader, the Text, the Poem: The Transactional Theory of the Literary Work.* Carbondale: Southern Illinois University Press, 1978.

Sartre, Jean-Paul. *What Is Literature? and Other Essays.* Cambridge, MA: Harvard University Press, 1988.

Wellek, Rene, and Austin Warren. *Theory of Literature.* San Diego: Harcourt Brace Jovanovich, 1977.

Winner, Ellen. *Invented Worlds: The Psychology of the Arts.* Cambridge, MA: Harvard University Press, 1982.

Poetry

recommended by Judith Wolinsky Steinbergh, author of "To Arrive in Another World: Poetry, Language Development, and Culture"

Dillard, Annie. *The Writing Life.* New York: Harper & Row, 1989.

Heard, Georgia. *For the Good of the Earth and the Sun: Teaching Poetry.* Portsmouth, NH: Heinemann, 1989.

Hopkins, Lee Bennett. *Pass the Poetry, Please!* New York: Harper & Row, 1972.

Johnson, David M. *Word Weaving: A Creative Approach to Teaching and Writing Poetry.* Urbana, IL: National Council of Teachers of English, 1990.

Kennedy, X. J., and Dorothy Kennedy. *Knock at a Star.* Boston: Little, Brown, 1982.

Koch, Kenneth. *Rose, Where Did You Get That Red?* New York: Random House, 1973.

Lewis, Claudia. *A Big Bite of the World.* Englewood Cliffs, NJ: Prentice-Hall, 1979.

Lewis, Richard. *Fire, Fire Burning Bright.* Six Cassettes for Young People on the Nature and Origin of Poetry. New York: The Touchstone Center.

Livingston, Myra Cohn. *The Child as Poet: Myth or Reality.* Boston: Horn Book, 1984.

Livingston, Myra Cohn. *Poem-Making: Ways to Begin Writing Poetry.* New York: Harper Collins, 1991.

McKim, Elizabeth, and Judith Wolinsky Steinbergh. *Beyond Words: Writing Poems with Children* (2nd ed.). Brookline, MA: Talking Stone Press, 1992.

Padgett, Ron (Ed.). *Handbook of Poetic Form.* New York: Teachers and Writers Collaborative, 1988.

Phillips, Ann. "Thinking on the Inside: Children's Poetry and Inner Speech." Unpublished paper. Cambridge, MA: Harvard Graduate School of Education, 1990.

Richardson, Elwyn. *In the Early World.* New York: Pantheon, 1964.

Robinson, Sandy. *Origins.* New York: Teachers and Writers Collaborative, 1989.

Stafford, William. *Writing the Australian Crawl.* Ann Arbor: University of Michigan Press, 1978.

Steinbergh, Judith Wolinsky. *A Living Anytime.* Boston: Talking Stone Press, 1988.

Steinbergh, Judith Wolinsky. "Writing Poems with Children." In *Reflections, The Brookline Educational Journal,* 7, 10–15, 1989.

Steinbergh, Judith, and Victor Cockburn. *Where I Come From! Songs and Poems from Many Cultures.* Brookline, MA: Talking Stone Press, 1991.

Teachers and Writers. Bimonthly publication of Teachers and Writers Collaborative, New York.

Tsujimoto, Joseph I. *Teaching Poetry Writing to Adolescents.* Urbana, IL: National Council of Teachers of English, 1964.

Zavatsky, Bill, and Ron Padgett (Eds.). *The Whole Word Catalogues I and II.* New York: McGraw-Hill, 1977.

Folk Music

recommended by Victor Cockburn, author of "The Uses of Folk Song and Songwriting in the Classroom"

Recordings

Alan Lomax Collectors Choice, Tradition 2057

Are We Almost There? Gentle Wind GW 1026

Ballads, Folkways 5251

Been in the Storm So Long: Spirituals and Shouts, Children's Game Songs and Folktales, Folkways 3842

Can We Go Now? Gentle Wind GW 1041
Child Ballads II, Caedmon TC 1145
Cisco Houston, Sonny Terry, and Brownie McGee, Folkways 31006
Feel Yourself in Motion, Talking Stone Productions TS 1002
Joan Baez, Vanguard 2077
Ledbelly (Huddie Ledbetter) Sings Folk Songs with Woody Guthrie, Malvina Reynolds,
  Cassandra CFS 2807
Music of the American Indians of the Southwest, Folkways 31006
Negro Prison Camp Work Songs (1951), Folkways 4475
Odetta Ballads and Blues, Tradition 1010
Pete Seeger Sings American Ballads, Folkways 2319
Pete Seeger Sings American Industrial Ballads, Folkways 5251
Pete Seeger Sings Woody Guthrie, Folkways 31002
Ramblin' Jack Eliot Sings Woody Guthrie, Prestige 7453
The Railroad in Folk Songs (1928–1940), RCA LPV 53
The Weavers Greatest Hits, Vanguard VSD 15/16
Troubadour: Original Songs and Poems for Children, Talking Stone Productions TS 1001

Music Books

Baggelaar, Kristin, and Donald Milton. *Folk Music: More Than a Song*. New York:
  Crowell, 1976.
Hart, Jane (Ed.). *Singing Bee! A Collection of Favorite Children's Songs*. New York:
  Lothrop, Lee & Shepard, 1982.
Seeger, Pete, and Bob Reiser. *Carry It On!* New York: Simon & Schuster, 1985.
Seeger, Ruth Crawford. *American Folk Songs for Children*. New York: Doubleday, 1948.

Philosophy of Arts

recommended by V. A. Howard, author of "And Practice Drives Me Mad; or, the
 Drudgery of Drill"

Cassirer, Ernst. *An Essay on Man*. New Haven, CT: Yale University Press, 1972.
Collingwood, R. G. *The Principles of Art*. New York: Oxford University Press, 1958.
Greene, Maxine. *Landscapes of Learning*. New York: Teachers College Press, 1978.
Hesse, Herman. *Magister Ludi* (or) *The Glass Bead Game*. New York: Bantam Books, 1969.
Howard, V. A. *Artistry: The Work of Artists*. Indianapolis: Hackett, 1982.
Read, Herbert E. *The Philosophy of Modern Art*. New York: Horizon Press, 1953.
Ryle, Gilbert. *The Concept of the Mind*. London: Hutchinson, 1963.
Schiller, Friedrich. *On the Aesthetic Education of Man*. Oxford: Clarendon Press, 1982.
Scruton, R. *Art and the Imagination*. London: Methuen, 1974.
Storrs, Anthony. *Solitude*. New York: Free Press, 1988.
Stravinsky, Igor. *The Poetics of Music*. Cambridge, MA: Harvard University Press, 1990.

Philosophy, Politics, Mysticism, and World Musics

recommended by James A. Hoffmann, author of "Computer-Aided Collaborative
 Music Instruction"

Attali, Jacques. *Noise: The Political Economy of Music* (trans. Brian Massumi).
  Minneapolis: University of Minnesota Press, 1985.
Frith, Simon, and Howard Horne. *Art into Pop*. New York: Methuen, 1987.
Godwin, Joscelyn. *Harmonies of Heaven and Earth: The Spiritual Dimensions of Music*.
  Rochester, VT: Inner Traditions International, 1987.

Godwin, Joscelyn. *Music, Mysticism and Magic.* New York: ARKANA, 1987.

Hamel, Peter Michael. *Through Music to the Self: How to Appreciate and Experience Music Anew* (trans. Peter Lemesurier). Boulder, CO: Shambhala, 1979.

Hart, Mickey. *Drumming at the Edge of Magic: A Journey into the Spirit of Percussion.* San Francisco: Harper, 1990.

Leppert, Richard, and Susan McClary (Eds.). *Music and Society: The Politics of Composition, Performance and Reception.* New York: Cambridge University Press, 1987.

Malm, William P. *Japanese Music and Musical Instruments.* Rutland, VT: Charles E. Tuttle, 1959.

Popley, H. A. *The Music of India* (3rd ed.). Boston: Crescendo, 1966.

Schafer, R. Murray. *The Tuning of the World.* New York: Alfred A. Knopf, 1977.

World Musics

recommended by Marie F. McCarthy, reviewer of *Music, Mind, and Education* by Keith Swanwick

Surveys of World Music

Malm, William P. *Music Cultures of the Pacific, the Near East, and Asia* (2nd ed.). Englewood Cliffs, NJ: Prentice-Hall, 1977.

May, Elizabeth (Ed.). *Music of Many Cultures.* Berkeley: University of California Press, 1980.

Nettl, Bruno. *Folk and Traditional Music of the Western Continents.* Englewood Cliffs, NJ: Prentice-Hall, 1973.

Sadie, Stanley (Ed.). *The New Grove Dictionary of Music and Musicians.* London: Macmillan, 1980.

Titon, Jeff (Ed.). *Worlds of Music.* New York: Schirmer Books, 1984.

World Musics in the Classroom

Adzinyah, Abraham K., Dumsani Maraire, and Judith Cook Tucker. *Let Your Voice Be Heard! Songs from Ghana and Zimbabwe.* Danbury, CT: World Music Press, 1984.

Amoaku, W. K. *African Songs and Rhythms for Children: Orff Schulwerk in the African Tradition.* New York: Schott Music, 1971. (Companion tape from Smithsonian/Folkways Records)

Anderson, William M. *Teaching Asian Music in Elementary and Secondary Schools: An Introduction to the Musics of India and Indonesia.* Danbury, CT: World Music Press, 1975.

Anderson, William M., and Joy E. Lawrence. *Integrating Music into the Classroom* (2nd ed.). Belmont, CA: Wadsworth, 1991.

Anderson, William M., and Patricia Shehan Campbell (Eds.). *Multicultural Perspectives in Music Education.* Reston, VA: Music Educators National Conference, 1989. (see Book Note)

Ballard, Louis W. *American Indian Music for the Classroom.* Phoenix, AZ: Canyon Records, 1973.

Burnett, Millie. *Dance Down the Rain, Sing Up the Corn: American Indian Chants and Games for Children.* Allisoni Park, PA: Music Innovations, 1975.

George, Luvenia A. *Teaching the Music of Six Different Cultures* (rev. ed.). Danbury, CT: World Music Press, 1987.

Jessup, Lynne. *World Music: A Source Book for Teaching.* Danbury, CT: World Music Press, 1988.

Jones, Bessie, and Bess Lomax Hawes. *Step It Down: Games, Plays, Songs, and Stories from the Afro-American Heritage.* Athens: University of Georgia Press, 1972.
Music in World Cultures. *Music Educators Journal,* Special Issue, October 1972.
Shehan, Patricia K. *Multicultural Music.* Morristown, NJ: Silver Burdett & Ginn, 1988.
Shehan Campbell, Patricia. *Lessons from the World: A Cross-Cultural Guide to Music Teaching and Learning.* New York: Schirmer Books, 1991.
The Multicultural Imperative. *Music Educators Journal,* May 1983, pp. 26–70.

Recommendations from Project Zero, Harvard University

by codirectors Howard Gardner, author of *To Open Minds: Chinese Clues to the Dilemma of Contemporary Education* (see Essay Review), and David Perkins

Gardner, Howard. *Art Education and Human Development.* Los Angeles: Getty Center for Education in the Arts, 1990.
Gardner, Howard. *Artful Scribbles.* New York: Basic Books, 1980.
Gardner, Howard. *The Arts and Human Development.* New York: Wiley, 1973.
Gardner, Howard. *To Open Minds: Chinese Clues to the Dilemma of Contemporary Education.* New York: Basic Books, 1989.
Perkins, David. *The Mind's Best Work.* Cambridge, MA: Harvard University Press, 1981.
Winner, Ellen. *Invented Worlds: A Psychology of the Arts.* Cambridge, MA: Harvard University Press, 1982.

EDITORS' CHOICES

Aesthetic Education

Hospers, John (Ed.). *Introductory Readings in Aesthetics.* New York: Free Press, 1969.
Kaelin, E. F. *An Aesthetics for Art Educators.* New York: Teachers College Press, 1989.

Arts and Creative Therapy

Furth, Gregg M. *The Secret World of Drawings: Healing through Art.* Boston: Sigo Press, 1988.
Podolsky, Edward. *Music Therapy.* New York: Philosophical Library, 1954.
Available from MMB Music, St. Louis, MO
Clark, Cynthia, and Donna Chadwick. *Clinically Adapted Instruments for the Multiply Handicapped,* 1980.
Guide to the Selection of Musical Instruments with Respect to Physical Ability and Disability (Developed by the Kardon Institute and the Moss Rehabilitation Center), 1982
Lee, Matthew. *Rehabilitation, Music and Human Well-Being,* 1989.
Nordoff, Paul, and Clyve Robbins. *Music Therapy in Special Education,* 1983.
Robbins, Clyve, and Carol Robbins. *Music for the Hearing Impaired,* 1980.
Standley, Jayne. *Music Techniques in Therapy Counseling and Special Education,* 1991.

Arts and Psychology

Bamberger, Jeanne. *The Mind behind the Musical Ear.* Cambridge, MA: Harvard University Press, 1991.

Boardman, Eunice (Ed.). *Dimensions of Musical Thinking.* Reston, VA: Music Educators National Conference, 1989. (see Book Note)

Gardner, Howard, and David Perkins (Eds.). *Art, Mind and Education: Research from Project Zero.* Chicago: University of Illinois Press, 1989. (see Book Note)

Meyer, Leonard B. *Emotion and Meaning in Music.* Chicago: University of Chicago Press, 1956.

Moody, William J. (Ed.). *Artistic Intelligences: Implications for Education.* New York: Teachers College Press, 1990. (see Book Note)

Sarason, Seymour. *The Challenge of Art to Psychology.* New Haven, CT: Yale University Press, 1988.

Spitz, Ellen Handler. *Art and Psyche.* New Haven, CT: Yale University Press, 1985.

Swanwick, Keith. *Music, Mind, and Education.* New York: Routledge, 1988. (see Book Review)

Walker, Robert. *Musical Beliefs: Psychological, Mythical, and Educational.* New York: Teachers College Press, 1990.

Dance

Brinson, Peter. *Dance as Education: Towards a National Dance Culture.* New York: Falmer Press, 1991.

Fraser, Diane Lynch. *Playdancing.* Pennington, NJ: Princeton Book, 1991. (see Book Note)

Haselbach, Barbara. *Dance Education: Basic Principles and Models for Nursery and Primary Schools.* New York: Schott, 1978.

Haskins, James. *Black Dance in America.* New York: Thomas Crowell, 1990.

Knowles, Patricia, and Rona Sande. *Dance Education in American Public Schools.* Urbana, IL: Council for Research in Music Education, 1991.

Long, Richard A. *The Black Tradition in American Dance.* New York: Rizzoli, 1990.

Thorpe, Edward. *Black Dance.* Woodstock, NY: Overlook Press, 1990.

Folk Art

Lipman, Jean. *American Folk Art in Wood, Metal and Stone.* New York: Pantheon, 1948.

Livingston, Jane. *Black Folk Art in America.* Jackson: University Press of Mississippi, 1982.

Oettinger, Marion, Jr. *Folk Treasures of Mexico: N. Rockefeller Collection.* New York: Abrams, 1990.

Twelker, Nancyann J. *Women and Their Quilts.* Bothell, WA: That Patchwork Place, 1988.

Ungerleider-Mayerson, Joy. *Jewish Folk Art.* New York: Summit Books, 1986.

Vlach, John Michael. *Afro-American Tradition in Decorative Arts.* Athens: University of Georgia Press, 1990.

Whiteford, Andrew H. *Southwestern Indian Baskets.* Santa Fe, NM: School of American Research Press, 1988.

Imagination, Improvisation, and Creativity

Copland, Aaron. *Music and Imagination.* Cambridge, MA: Harvard University Press, 1952.

Gardner, Howard. *Art, Mind & Brain: A Cognitive Approach to Creativity.* New York: Basic Books, 1982.

Ghiselin, Brewster (Ed.). *The Creative Process.* Berkeley: University of California Press, 1985.

John-Steiner, Vera. *Notebooks of the Mind: Explorations of Thinking.* New York: Harper & Row, 1985.

Kagan, Jerome (Ed.). *Creativity and Learning.* Boston: Houghton Mifflin, 1967.
Nachmanovitch, Stephen. *Free Play: Improvisation in Life and Art.* Los Angeles: Jeremy P. Tarcher, 1990. (see Book Note)
Wallace, Doris B., and Howard E. Gruber (Eds.). *Creative People at Work: Twelve Cognitive Case Studies.* New York: Oxford University Press, 1989.
Warnock, Mary. *Imagination.* Berkeley: University of California Press, 1978.

Literature

Cheung, King-kok, and Stan Yogi. *Asian American Literature: An Annotated Bibliography.* New York: Modern Language Association of America, 1988.
Emanuel, James A., and Theodore L. Gross. *Dark Symphony: Negro Literature in America.* New York: Free Press, 1968.
Gates, Louis, Jr. (Ed.). *Reading Black, Reading Feminist: A Critical Anthology.* New York: Meridan, 1990. (see Book Note)
Gilbert, Sandra M., and Susan Gubar (Eds.). *No Man's Land: The Place of the Woman Writer in the Twentieth Century: Vol. I. The War of the Words; Vol. II. Sexchanges.* New Haven, CT: Yale University Press, 1989. (see Book Note)
Kalechofsky, Robert, and Roberta Kalechofsky (Eds.). *The Global Anthology of Jewish Women Writers.* Marblehead, MA: Micah Publications, 1990. (see Book Note)
Kim, Elaine H. *Asian American Literature: An Introduction to the Writings and Their Social Context.* Philadelphia: Temple University Press, 1982.
Ling, Amy. *Between Worlds: Women Writers of Chinese Ancestry.* New York: Pergamon Press, 1990.
Stevick, Philip (Ed.). *Anti-Story: An Anthology of Experimental Fiction.* New York: Free Press, 1971.
Stevick, Philip (Ed.). *The Theory of the Novel.* New York: Free Press, 1967.

Music

Carawan, Guy, and Candie Carawan. *Sing for Freedom: The Story of the Civil Rights Movement through Its Songs.* Bethlehem, PA: A Sing Out Publication, 1990.
Ellis, Catherine. *Aboriginal Music: Education for Living.* St. Lucia: University of Queensland Press, 1985/1989.
Hoffer, Charles R. *Teaching Music in the Secondary Schools* (4th ed.). Belmont, CA: Wadsworth, 1991. (see Book Note)
Jezic, Diane Peacock. *Women Composers: The Lost Tradition Found.* New York: Feminist Press, 1988. (see Book Note)
Rubin, Ruth. *Voices of a People: The Story of Yiddish Folksong.* Philadelphia: Jewish Publication Society of America, 1979.
Schafer, R. Murray. *Creative Music Education.* New York: Schirmer Books, 1976.

Performers and Performing

Fowler, Charles (Ed.). *The Crane Symposium: Toward an Understanding of the Teaching and Learning of Music Performance.* Potsdam: Potsdam College of the State University of New York, 1988.
Guidelines for Performances of School Music Groups. Reston, VA: Music Educators National Conference, 1986.
Kammerman, Jack B., and Rosanne Martoella. *Performers and Performances: The Social Organization of Artistic Work.* Westport, CT: Bergin & Garvey, 1983.

Ristad, Eloise. *A Soprano on Her Head: Right-Side-Up Reflections on Life and Other Performances*. Moab, UT: Real People Press, 1982.

Schechner, Richard. *Performance Theory*. New York: Routledge, 1988.

Schechner, Richard, and Willa Appel (Eds.). *By Means of Performance*. New York: Cambridge University Press, 1990.

Turner, Victor. *The Anthropology of Performance*. New York: PAJ Publications, 1986.

Philosophy

Coomaraswamy, Ananda K. *The Transformation of Nature in Art*. New York: Dover, 1956.

Greene, Maxine. *The Dialectic of Freedom*. New York: Teachers College Press, 1988.

Hospers, John. *Understanding the Arts*. Englewood Cliffs, NJ: Prentice-Hall, 1982.

Howard, V. A. *Learning by All Means: Lessons from Philosophy*. New York: Peter Lang, 1992.

Langer, Susanne. *Philosophy in a New Key: A Study in Symbolism of Reason, Rite and Art*. Cambridge, MA: Harvard University Press, 1979.

Leppert, Richard (Ed.). *Music and Society*. New York: Cambridge University Press, 1987.

Reimer, Bennett. *A Philosphy of Music Education*. Englewood Cliffs, NJ: Prentice-Hall, 1989.

Small, Christopher. *Music, Society, Education*. London: John Calder, 1977.

Smith, Ralph. *The Sense of Art: A Study in Aesthetic Education*. New York: Routledge, 1989.

Policy, Research, and Reform

Arian, Edward. *The Unfulfilled Promise: Public Subsidy of the Arts in America*. Philadelphia: Temple University Press, 1989.

Balfe, Judith H., and Cherbo Heine (Eds.). *Arts Education beyond the Classroom*. New York: American Council for the Arts, 1988.

Blandy, Doug, and Kristin Congdon. *Art in a Democracy*. New York: Teachers College Press, 1987. (see Book Note)

Fowler, Charles. *Can We Rescue the Arts for America's Children? Coming to Our Senses — 10 Years Later*. New York: American Council for the Arts, 1988.

Growing Up Complete: The Imperative for Music Education. Reston, VA: Music Educators National Conference, 1991. (see Book Note)

Leonard, Charles. *The Status of Arts Education in American Public Schools*. Urbana, IL: Council for Research in Music Education, 1991.

McLaughlin, John (Ed.). *A Guide to National and State Arts Education Services*. New York: American Council for the Arts, 1987.

McLaughlin, John T. (Ed.). *Toward a New Era in Arts Education: The Interlochen Symposium*. New York: American Council for the Arts, 1988.

Pankratz, David, and Kevin Mulcahy. *The Challenge to Reform Arts Education: What Role Can Research Play?* New York: American Council for the Arts, 1989. (see Book Note)

Quinn, Thomas, and Cheryl Hanks (Eds.). *Coming to Our Senses: The Significance of the Arts for American Education*. New York: American Council for the Arts, 1977.

Remer, Jane. *Changing Schools through the Arts*. New York: American Council for the Arts, 1982/1990.

Why We Need the Arts: Eight Quotable Speeches by Leaders in Education, Government, Business and the Arts. New York: American Council for the Arts, 1989.

Theater and Film

Berson, Misha (Ed.). *Between Worlds: Contemporary Asian American Plays.* New York: Theatre Communications Group, 1990.

Case, Sue-Ellen. *Feminism and Theatre.* New York: Methuen, 1988.

Dyer, Richard. *Now You See It: Studies on Lesbian and Gay Film.* New York: Routledge, 1990.

Ellsworth, Elizabeth, and Mariamne H. Whatley. *The Ideology of Images in Educational Media: Hidden Curriculums in the Classroom.* New York: Teachers College Press, 1990.

Epskamp, Kees P. *Theatre in Search of Social Change: The Relative Significance of Different Theatrical Approaches* (CESO Paperback No. 7). The Hague: Centre for the Study of Education in Developing Countries, 1989. (see Book Note)

Hatch, James V. (Ed.). *Black Theatre USA: 45 Plays by Black Americans, 1847–1974.* New York: Free Press, 1974.

Watson, Robert. *Film & Television in Education: An Aesthetic Approach to the Moving Image.* New York: Falmer Press, 1990.

Visual Arts

Chaplik, Dorothy. *Latin American Art: An Introduction to the Works of the 20th Century.* Jefferson, NC: McFarland, 1989. (see Book Note)

Chipp, Herschel B. *Theories of Modern Art: A Source Book by Artists and Critics.* Los Angeles: University of California Press, 1969.

Edwards, Betty. *Drawing on the Right Side of the Brain.* Los Angeles: Jeremy P. Tarcher, 1989.

Elfand, Arthur D. *A History of Art Education: Intellectual and Social Currents in Teaching the Visual Arts.* New York: Teachers College Press, 1990. (see Book Note)

Engel, Peter. *Folding the Universe: Origami from Angelfish to Zen.* New York: Vintage, 1989.

Goldwater, Robert, and Marco Treves (Eds.). *Artists on Art: From the XIV to the XX Century.* New York: Pantheon, 1942/1972.

Goodnow, Jacqueline. *Children Drawing.* Cambridge, MA: Harvard University Press, 1977.

Kingery, W. David, and Pamela B. Vandiver. *Ceramic Masterpieces: Art, Structure, Technology.* New York: Free Press, 1986.

Pollack, Griselda. *Vision and Difference: Femininity, Feminism and the Histories of Art.* New York: Routledge, 1988.

Szekely, George. *Encouraging Creativity in Art Lessons.* New York: Teachers College Press, 1988.

Volavkova, Hana (Ed.). *I Never Saw Another Butterfly: Children's Drawings and Poems from Terezin Concentration Camp, 1942–1944.* New York: McGraw-Hill, 1971.

With Children in Mind

Dorros, Arthur. *Tonight is Carnaval.* New York: Dutton Children's Books, 1991.

Fleischman, Paul. *Joyful Noise: Poems for Two Voices.* New York: Harper & Row, 1988.

Jarnow, Jill. *All Ears: How to Choose and Use Recorded Music for Children.* New York: Penguin Books, 1991. (see Book Note)

Music for Children: Orff-Schulwerk American Edition (Vol. 2, primary; Vol. 3, upper elementary). New York: Schott Music, 1977.

Wright, Susan (Ed.). *The Arts in Early Childhood.* Englewood Cliffs, NJ: Prentice-Hall, 1991.

Available from Harper Collins, New York, NY (1991)
Hoberman, Mary Ann, and Malcah Zeldis. *A Fine Fat Pig and Other Animal Poems.*
Kipling, Rudyard. *Just So Stories,* woodcuts by David Frampton.
Lattimore, Deborah Nourse. *The Sailor Who Captured the Sea: A Story of the Book of Kells.*
Schwartz, Howard, and Barbara Rush. *The Diamond Tree: Jewish Tales From Around the World,* illustrated by Uri Shulevitz.
Winthrop, Elizabeth (adapted by). *Vasilissa the Beautiful: A Russian Folktale,* illustrated by Alexander Koshkin.

JOURNALS

Amerasia Journal, Los Angeles, CA
Annual Review of Jazz Studies, New Brunswick, NJ
Arts and the Islamic World, London, England
Arts Education Policy Review, Indianapolis, IN
Asian Music, New York, NY
Black American Literature Forum, Terre Haute, IN
Black Art, Claremont, CA
Black Arts Annual, New York, NY
Craft History, Bath, England
Cultural Views, Cambridge, MA
Design for Arts in Education, Indianapolis, IN
Down Beat, Elmhurst, IL
Eastern Art Report, London, England
Electronic Musician, Oklahoma City, OK
Folklore and Mythology Studies, Los Angeles, CA
International Review of African American Art, Santa Monica, CA
Jazz Journal International, London, England
Journal of Aesthetic Education, Champaign, IL
Journal of Aesthetics and Art Criticism, Philadelphia, PA
Journal of American Drama and Theatre, New York, NY
Journal of Experimental Aesthetics, Vancouver, Canada
Journal of Music Therapy, Washington, DC
Journal of Research in Music Education, Reston, VA
Journal of the Theory and Criticism of the Visual Arts, Tempe, AZ
Living Blues, University, MI
Music Educator's Journal, Reston, VA
National Association of Jazz Educators (NAJE) Educator, Manhattan, KS
Sing Out, New York, NY
Stern's Performing Arts Directory, New York, NY
Women and Performance, New York, NY

NATIONAL ARTS EDUCATION AND SERVICE ORGANIZATIONS

American Association of Theatre for
  Youth
c/o Theatre Arts Dept.
203 Performing Arts Building
Blacksburg, VA 24061
(703) 961-7624

American Council for the Arts
1285 Avenue of the Americas
Floor 3, Area M
New York, NY 10019
(212) 245-4510

Dance USA
633 E Street NW
Washington, DC 20004
(202) 628-0144

Getty Center for Education in the Arts
1875 Century Park East, No. 2300
Los Angeles, CA 90067
(213) 277-9188

Harvard Project Zero
Harvard Graduate School of Education
Longfellow Hall
13 Appian Way
Cambridge, MA 02138
(617) 495-4342

International Thespian Society
3368 Central Parkway
Cincinnati, OH 45225-2392
(513) 559-1996

Kennedy Center Alliance for Arts
  Education
Kennedy Center for the Performing Arts
Washington, DC 20566
(202) 254-7190

Museum of American Folk Art
2 Lincoln Square
New York, NY 10023

Music Educators National Conference
1902 Association Drive
Reston, VA 22091
(703) 860-4000

National Art Education Association
1916 Association Drive
Reston, VA 22091
(703) 860-8000

National Arts Education Research Center
University of Illinois at Urbana-
  Champaign
1114 West Nevada Street
Urbana, IL 61801
(217) 333-1027

National Dance Association
1900 Association Drive
Reston, VA 22091
(703) 476-3421

National Endowment for the Arts
1100 Pennsylvania Avenue NW
Washington, DC 20506
(202) 682-5426

National Foundation for Advancement
  in the Arts
100 North Biscayne Blvd., No. 1801
Miami, FL 33132
(305) 371-9470

Opera America
633 E Street NW
Washington, DC 20004
(202) 347-9262

Very Special Arts
Kennedy Center for the Performing Arts
Washington, DC 20566
(202) 662-8899

Young Audiences
115 East 92nd Street
New York, NY 10128
(212) 831-8110

About the Editors

MERRYL RUTH GOLDBERG is an instructor of education at the Harvard Graduate School of Education and teaches cognitive development at Wheelock College, Boston, Massachusetts. She is also a professional saxophonist with the Klezmer Conservatory Band. Her publications include "Teaching and Learning: A Collaborative Process" in *Music Educators Journal* (1990) and "Expressing and Assessing Understanding through the Arts" in *Phi Delta Kappan* (1992).

ANN PHILLIPS is a fifth-grade teacher in Brookline, Massachusetts, and a member of the Brookline Teacher Researcher Seminar. Her professional interests include the arts and epistemology of teaching and learning, classroom discourse, and teacher research. Her articles include "What Teachers Need to Know" (1989) and "Raising the Teacher's Voice: The Ironic Role of Silence" (forthcoming), two technical reports by the Literacies Institute.

About the Contributors

BARBARA BECKWITH, a former teacher, is a writer specializing in education. She is also Vice President for External Organizing of the National Writers Union. Her publications include *Standing up to the SAT* (with J. Weiss and R. Schaeffer, 1989).

VICTOR COCKBURN, an artist-educator, is Artistic Director of Troubadour, a collaborative, curriculum-related program for teachers and students in which he uses folk song as an educational tool. In addition to writing songs and performing for children and adults, he produces tapes for educational projects. He is author of *Writing Songs in the Classroom: A Guide for the Non-Musical Teacher* (1989) and coproducer of *On the Trail*, a cassette recording of original poems and songs for children (with J. W. Steinbergh, 1991).

GARY DeCOKER is Assistant Professor in the Department of Education at Ohio Wesleyan University. Education in Japan and aesthetic education are his primary professional interests. He is author of "Secret Teachings in Medieval Calligraphy: *Jubokusho* and *Saiyosho*," in *Monumenta Nipponica* (1988), a translation and analysis of two treatises on the teaching of the art of calligraphy.

KAREN GALLAS, who teaches first and second grade in the Brookline (Massachusetts) Public Schools, is interested in developing and documenting multi-arts curricula. She also explores issues of multiple literacies in the classroom. Her articles include "Integrating the Arts in Rural Schools" in *The Rural Educator* (1986) and "When Children Take the Chair: A Study of Sharing Time in a Primary Classroom" in *Language Arts* (1992).

W. THOMPSON GARFIELD, a songwriter, storyteller, and visual artist, is Senior Staff Associate at Cooperative Artists Institute in Jamaica Plain, Massachusetts. He produces staff-development materials to help teachers use the arts to improve their learning environments. He is codeveloper of the Tribal Rhythms Program and has been a professional musician since 1964.

MARGOT GRALLERT has been a Humanities Consultant since 1971 at the McCarthy-Towne School in Acton, Massachusetts, and is an associate faculty member at Goddard College, Plainfield, Vermont. She is interested in working with artists in education, specifically with classroom teachers to help them understand artwork as a product of a thinking process through which their students can learn and communicate. She has made numerous presentations on the subject, including "Artistic Thinking as an Integrated Aspect of Learning" at the Harvard Graduate School of Education.

MAXINE GREENE is Professor of Philosophy and Education (Emeritus) at Columbia University Teachers College, where she holds the title of William F. Russell Professor in the Foundations of Education. Her professional interests include the arts, literature, and the humanities in contexts of philosophy and criticism. Her numerous publications include *Teacher as Stranger* (1974), *Landscapes of Learning* (1978), and *The Dialectic of Freedom* (1988).

JAMES A. HOFFMANN is a member of the Graduate and Undergraduate Theory Departments at the New England Conservatory of Music in Boston, Massachusetts. Since 1977 he has served as director of the New England Conservatory Enchanted Circle Concert Series, which he cofounded. He has published music for trombone and wind/brass ensembles, and is coauthor of "A Conversation with Gunther Schuller" in *Perspectives of New Music* (with J. G. Maneri, 1986).

CHARLES M. HOLLEY is cofounder and Senior Staff Associate of Cooperative Artists Institute, Jamaica Plain, Massachusetts, and codeveloper of the Tribal Rhythms Program. His major professional interests are to help young adults develop entrepreneurial skills and to develop resource materials with a multicultural focus to improve landlord-tenant relations. He is a sculptor, storyteller, musician, and community organizer with expertise in developing group problem-solving techniques.

V. A. HOWARD is Codirector of the Philosophy of Education Research Center at Harvard Graduate School of Education. His primary professional interests include aesthetics and education, symbolism and cognition, learning theory, and music education. His publications include *Varieties of Thinking: Essays from Harvard's Philosophy of Education Research Center* (1990), *Learning by All Means: Lessons from the Arts* (1992), and *Thinking Together: The Dialogue of Discovery* (1992).

J. CURTIS JONES is Senior Staff Associate and cofounder of Cooperative Artists Institute in Jamaica Plain, Massachusetts, and codeveloper of the Tribal Rhythms Program. A former classroom teacher, he is interested in the research and study of the use of socially patterned thought in education and therapy. He is a writer, storyteller, actor, educator, and musician, and is writing a book that focuses on removing oppressive institutions from the learning environment.

MARIE F. MCCARTHY is Assistant Professor of Music at Indiana University–Purdue University at Fort Wayne. Her professional interests are multicultural music education and comparative history of music education. She is author of "Music in Primary Education: Dispelling Myths, Identifying Values" in *An Muinteoir Naisiunta* [Irish Teachers Journal] (1989). Before coming to the United States on a Fulbright Scholarship, she was a national teacher with the Irish Department of Education.

KATHLEEN MURPHEY is Assistant Professor of Education at Indiana University–Purdue University at Fort Wayne. Her major professional interests are educational history, educational policy, and comparative education, with a focus on China. She is coauthor (with B. Gates and A. Reich, 1985) of " 'I Took My Childhood into My Hands': Some Voices from High School" in S. L. Rich and A. Phillips (Eds.), *Women's Education and Experience.* Her article on Johnetta Cole, president of Spelman College, is forthcoming in *Women Educators in the United States: A Biographical and Bibliographical Sourcebook.*

SUSAN E. PORTER, Senior Staff Associate at Cooperative Artists Institute in Jamaica Plain, Massachusetts, works with "at-risk" youth and children with special needs, using the arts to improve self-esteem. A former classroom teacher and educational materials developer, she is codeveloper of the Tribal Rhythms Program and coauthor of *The Citygames Book* (with D. Hanson, A. Bell, J. Zien, and F. Kresse, 1975). She is a visual artist and craftsperson who specializes in soft sculpture and wearable art.

JUDITH WOLINSKY STEINBERGH is a poet and teacher who performs, leads workshops, and creates tapes with Troubadour, a collaborative educational program of poetry and music for teachers and students. Her work focuses on the significance of poetry to the learning and expressive life of the developing child. She was Staff Writer-in-Residence in the Brookline (Massachusetts) Public Schools from 1986 to 1992, and has trained teachers throughout New England. She also develops curriculum for school systems and educational publishers. Her books include *Beyond Words: Writing Poems with Children* (with E. McKim, 1983) and *A Living Anytime* (1988).